Indian Territory

Surviving 160 Acres of Betrayal

A Tale of the Allotment Era

by
Tatianna Keblish Duncan

Research and storytelling supported by
The Lucinda Hickory Research Institute
Owasso, Oklahoma

ISBN: 979-8-9933923-0-1, paperback

ISBN: 979-8-9933923-1-8, hardcover

ISBN: 979-8-9933923-3-2, epub

Library of Congress Control Number: 2025924423

First Edition, 2025

Published by **Ndnfish2fry**
Printed in the United States of America

Dedication

Dedicated to all the American Indian descendants of the Allotment Era who carry their stories in silence—those who still search for answers to the questions left behind.

To our ancestors who fell victim to the deeds of dishonest men for which a state of corruption was born. We seek justice... as we continue the journey.

Sallie, Thomas, and Louina Hickory. This portrait shows Thomas Hickory with his daughters, Sallie and Louina. Together, they endured some of the harshest realities of the Allotment Era, forced to navigate a world that was unfamiliar and stacked against them. Much of the girls' youth was spent helping their father, who spoke only Creek, push back against guardians and grafters determined to seize their land — land that would fuel the rise of a wealthy Tulsa few Native families could share in.

Author's Note

While this work is rooted in the Indian experience of the Allotment Era, the Freedmen of the Creek Nation endured their own battles under the same corrupt system. Their stories, too, deserve to be told — by those to whom they rightfully belong.

Terminology used in this book reflects the language of the time and is not intended to offend or disparage any person or group.

This book began with the oral history my mother shared with us growing up:

"Those rich white people over there, with all the wealthy homes — stole our land."

A lifetime of questions and years of research led me to understand where "over there" is, and who "those rich white people" were. I've also come to see that while they may have benefited from our loss, most did not personally "steal" the land — though many still seek the "quieting of titles," which remains an open wound for descendants.

The poems and prose in between chapters are from my manifesto, *A Manifesto: 160 Acres of Betrayal*, written while preparing this book. Other epigraphs were written along the way or borrowed from other Native Americans whose words resound through these pages and contribute to this story.

"It is my desire that the government should let me alone until I could educate my children and prepare them to become citizens of the United States; prepare them for the change. I would be glad if the United States would keep faith with us. At this time, we are not prepared to take citizenship upon ourselves. We are not accustomed to their language."

— *Redbird of the Cherokees*

Preface

The Indian voice is often the last to be heard—and the first to be pitied. When I was growing up, I heard teachers say, "We should be ashamed of what we did to the Indians." I heard something similar at home: what was done to the Indians. I also knew I was one of them—an Indian. But no one ever said exactly what was done.

There was the Trail of Tears, yes, but what I heard whispered at home was something different, something shrouded in mystery which left me in confusion.

Years of research later, I've learned something else: no one really wants to know what happened. If you're Indian, you might think you already know. But as I've spoken with others, I realized they didn't know—or at least, they didn't convince me they knew.

If you're part of Tulsa, you might not want to know. To know could mean lawsuits. White Tulsa has its own oral history too. Tribal Nations are empathetic, but unwilling—or unable—to take action.

I've always felt that was a failure on my part, that I didn't help them understand what actually happened. I thought they already knew. But if they did know then how could they not take action? If they knew and did nothing... what does that mean?

And so, I began to realize: no one really wants to know about Indians, Native Americans, Indigenous people—unless we're beading earrings, stomping to our religion, or frying bread... which, by the way, is a new tradition—much like Spam.

If we are telling our truths, we are treated like troublemakers, because we are Indians, and our voices still don't really matter—not to them.

This book is my attempt to break that silence. To speak where others were silenced. To tell what was done to the Indians, and honor those who lived it.

"If we don't tell our story, someone else will.
They'll get it wrong—
and people will believe them."
— *Tatianna K. Duncan*, *Mvskoke/Cherokee Native*

Acknowledgements

To my husband, Christopher Duncan, who has never questioned how important this journey is to me, and whose relentless support and unwavering belief have carried me through.

To my parents — my dad, for always supporting Native culture (may he rest in peace), and my mother, who so passionately shared her lived experiences along with the stories she carried from my grandmother and the generations before her.

To my children—*Natasha Hickory Rogers Keblish*, who always wondered why I didn't start this sooner. I am grateful for your support. *Christopher Edward Duncan II*, who challenged me with the hard questions which pushed me forward. *Felicia Louina Duncan,* whose endless and unwavering support sustains me. Mvto / Wado / Thank you.

To my sister, Scooter, for taking the time to talk through these stories with me, even when the conversations weren't easy — your willingness to engage means more than you know. And to my other siblings, who shared the same space as we listened to these stories together, your presence in those moments is part of this book's foundation.

To JD Colbert — without whose work this book would not have been possible. JD has been advocating for the ancestors of the Allotment Era far longer than most have even known this history existed, ensuring their stories are told with truth and respect. His ability to navigate and succeed in the wake of forced assimilation is a testament to his strength, vision, and unwavering dedication to excellence, and it has been a source of inspiration for me. As a mentor, he has taught me much — especially how to maneuver in a world that too often works against Indian voices like ours.

To my cousins — especially Gary Worsham, whose steadfast support and inspiration have been with me from the very beginning, and his daughters, Jessica and Erica, who have shown genuine interest and pride in this journey. And to all my other cousins who have offered personal support and shared their own stories and trauma — this is something we hold in common. There are too many of you to name, but please know I carry your encouragement with me on every page.

To my Board of Directors and Advisors — my cousin, Dr. DeAnaLisa Jones, Annette Arkeetta, Dr. Gale Justin and, Dr. Russell Cobb — each of whom has been only a phone call away with wisdom and support, and to whom I extend my deepest gratitude. To my trusted advisors, past and present, whose insight has helped shape both the vision and direction of this work — and to Gano Perez, a true plank owner of LHRI, who always shows up and offers his expertise, support and friendship at every event and meeting.

The Oklahoma Historical Society and their digital archive, *The Gateway to Oklahoma History*, have been invaluable to my research. Many of the newspaper articles that shaped this book, whether quoted directly or part of the broader narrative, came from their collection. These preserved records, once scattered and nearly forgotten, helped illuminate the stories of my ancestors and the shadowy truths of the Allotment Era.

Many sources made this work possible, and the National Archives at Fort Worth stands among the most important. Their staff's commitment to preservation and accessibility made it possible to reconstruct the history that unfolds in these pages.

To the many along the way who shared their stories and experiences.

To Jim and Robin Tilly — thank you for reading my early words, meeting me for lunch, and helping me shape what became this historical memoir.

To Brittany Harlow Tidwell and Kelley Tidwell for their role in the Stealing Tvlse series and for organizing the Summer Research Tour to NARA archives in Fort Worth, Lenexa, and Philadelphia.

To the non-Natives who tried to be supportive, even when you could not fully see the vision I carried — I still appreciate your efforts to move this story forward, whatever your motives may have been.

And again, the most heartfelt thanks to my husband, Christopher Edward Duncan — whose support, both financial and emotional, and whose own lived experiences as an African American, have kept me grounded in the broader injustices this country has inflicted on so many. His presence has kept me steady and strong as I brought this story to life—*all my heart, all my love, always.*

Table of Contents

PROLOGUE: I

ON AN OKLAHOMA STORMY NIGHT I

WAITING FOR THEM WERE TWO MEN, COLD, STERN, AND UNINVITED... I
160 acres of betrayal... 4

CHAPTER 1 1

GENERATIONAL TRAUMA 1

A MOTHER'S LOVE 1
There was conflict... 8

FAMILY TREE 9

CHAPTER 2 11

WE CALLED IT TVLSE (TULSA) 11

FROM GREAT CREEK WARRIOR TO THE IMPROVIDENT INDIAN 11

CHAPTER 3 23

TUCKABACHE 23

LAST GENERATION OF GREAT CREEK WARRIORS 23
The Council Oak Tree 29

CHAPTER 4 31

THE DEATH OF TUCKABACHE 31

THE THREE WHITE MEN AND THE WILL 31
Land Ownership 43
Remembering Tuckabache 44

CHAPTER 5 47

THE PROBATE BATTLE 47

THE COCONUT SHELL GAME BEGINS! 47
The Swindle... 51

CHAPTER 6 53

THE DANGER OF BEING INDIAN DURING ALLOTMENT: 53

NAME: TOM CONEY CAUSE OF DEATH: FEVER TYPE: UNKNOWN 53
The Guardian 63

CHAPTER 7 65

FOREVER YOUNG – LUCINDA 65

GONE TOO SOON 65
"Remembering Jennie" 76
Allotment... 78

CHAPTER 8 79

THE DEMISE OF SAM DAVIS 79

AND WHOSE OLIVER? 79

CHAPTER 9 89

LOUINA & THE PROMISE 89

HER MOM'S DYING WISH 89
That is why... 97

CHAPTER 10 99

IN WALKS POO SUNDAY 99

TAKING A STAND FOR HIS FAMILY 99
Moving forward... 102

CHAPTER 11 103

THE FAMILY HOME **103**

IT WASN'T JUST SWINDLE, IT WAS OUTRIGHT THEFT 103
And the graft was on... *108*

CHAPTER 12 .... **109**

DOSES OF BETRAYAL **109**

THE BUSINESS OF KILLING INDIANS FOR LAND 109
The Spirit of the Indian Family Attacked *112*

CHAPTER 13 .... **113**

"FRIENDS OF THE INDIAN" OR "DEAD INDIAN" **113**

KILL THE INDIAN, SAVE THE MAN KILL THE INDIAN, TAKE THE LAND .. 113
The legacy of my ancestors... .... *119*

CHAPTER 14 .... **121**

THOMAS HICKORY **121**

A TALE OF THE ALLOTMENT ERA... 121

CHAPTER 15 .... **127**

BOOMERS, SOONERS, AND BROKEN PROMISES................ **127**

A STATE BUILT ON CORRUPTION 127

CHAPTER 16 .... **139**

THE COST OF COURAGE: **139**

IT'S TIME TO MOVE ON.. 139

CHAPTER 17 .... **147**

THEY WERE NOT SILENT—THEY WERE SILENCED **147**

AS THE BATTLE RAGES ON... 147
The Crime of 1908..... *151*

CHAPTER 18 153

THE CRIME OF 1908.. 153

THE IMPOSITION OF COLONIZATION 153

CHAPTER 19 159

THE HOPE OF RECOVERY 159

SURVIVING 160 ACRES OF BETRAYAL.. 159

Remembering Louina.................................... 164

CHAPTER 20 169

CUSTODIANS OF CORRUPTION 169

THE DARK REALITY OF THE ALLOTMENT ERA. 169

The Inheritance... 174

CHAPTER 21 175

SMOKE FOLLOWS BEAUTY 175

THE FINAL YEARS OF THOMAS HICKORY....................................... 175

Today 182

Remembering the Allotment Era 183

CHAPTER 22 187

IN THE ASHES OF THE AFTERMATH 187

WE CARE AND WE SHALL REFER: TULSA'S UNPLEASANT HISTORY 187

EPILOGUE 197

AFTERWORD 199

THE JOURNEY CONTINUES... 199

TATIANNA 203

ABOUT THE AUTHOR 203

INDIAN TERRITORY: 160 ACRES OF BETRAYAL 205

GLOSSARY.. 205

DOCUMENTS OF EVIDENCE AND CITATIONS 212

ON AN OKLAHOMA STORMY NIGHT

Waiting for them were two men,
cold, stern, and uninvited

Two men from Tulsa gave no regard to the "Oklahoma stormy night" or to the two young girls fast asleep, at St. Elizabeth's Catholic Boarding School for Indians in Purcell, Oklahoma. They had come for Louina & Sallie Hickory, minor Creek girls who carried the weight of protecting their family's land from speculators.

"Louina, Sallie—you have visitors outside," the Reverend Mother said, waking them out of their sleep. "They say it's important that they need to speak with you tonight."

What could it be now? Louina felt her stomach twist into a knot as she reached for Sallie's hand.

Bewildered and frightened, the girls stepped into the storm. Their mother, Jennie, and sister Lucinda had died suddenly without cause or answers. With their father and younger brother still at home, they had every reason to be concerned.

As they opened the door to the Oklahoma stormy night, the wind howled through the trees, rain poured down in sheets. Waiting for them, were two men: cold, stern, and uninvited.

They weren't there out of concern. They intended to force the young, frightened girls to sign away their land.

Faced with fear and intimidation, the girls were told they'd lose everything if they didn't sign.

I don't know exactly what happened that night. The oral history stopped there. But I do know this: they spent the rest of their youth fighting their guardian Dr. JCW Bland, the real estate developer J.O. Campbell, attorney James H. Sykes, and the local courts who sought out the Hickory's to force the sale of their home.

Hearing this story, I was alarmed about how the two young girls felt, being pulled from their beds into the storm, and threatened with the loss of everything.

After all they had already experienced, they knew the depravity of these types of grafters.

The Hickory story is just one truth in the dark reality of the Allotment Era, a time of calculated betrayal against Native families across Oklahoma. Children were sent away. Elders were swindled. Land was stolen through what are called legal loopholes, guardianships, threats, and violence.

Not much of it seemed legal to me as I have gained insight into foul play that led to the death of many of my land-holding ancestors.

The story being told in this book is of just one "Indian family" of Tvlse (Tulsa), Oklahoma. But to be clear, this is an "Indian" story, and it happened to many families within all tribes across Indian Territory. We will see how injustice unfolds *for full-bloods* like the Hickory family. And even now, justice hasn't come for the crimes committed against Indians, people who asked for nothing more than the right to live in peace on their own land.

This is a true story of dispossession, survival, and generational trauma told from the bloodline of those who endured it.

160 acres of betrayal...

160 acres is what we got,
in the Mvskoke Nation
on the Mvskoke Reservation.

160 acres is what they stole,
in the Mvskoke Nation
on the Mvskoke Reservation.

Chapter 1

GENERATIONAL TRAUMA

A mother's love

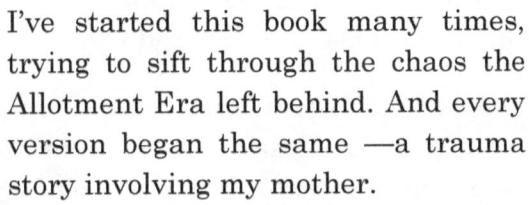

I've started this book many times, trying to sift through the chaos the Allotment Era left behind. And every version began the same —a trauma story involving my mother.

A Creek/Cherokee Native, mom is not only a woman of remarkable talents, she is dynamic and beautiful, with a creativity that transformed everything she touched. As a seamstress, her ideas became masterpieces. Her desserts are a work of art you couldn't wait to eat but made you think twice if you should even touch her creations. They were beautiful!

She could also organize chaos like no one I've ever known, transforming the ordinary into the extraordinary. Her laughter could fill a room, and her anger could silence one.

Born in 1939, she grew up in the aftermath of the Allotment Era. Though the official policies had ended, her life was shaped by the consequences of that corruption. The death of her mother, Louina Sunday née Hickory, when she was just 12 years old, no doubt left a deep wound that would never fully heal. She was left to navigate a world already shattered by greed and betrayal, a world shaped long before her birth.

The Allotment Era had broken families by enabling land theft that robbed children of stability. I'm not sure she knew how shattered it truly was—but she knew what it felt like—the fear, the loss, and the mistrust. Whether she could name the system or not, she lived inside its damage. And after her mother died, that damage became personal and inescapable.

My mother understood the injustices inflicted on our "American Indian" ancestors by colonizers, though she would've just said "white people."

I've come to believe it's time we make some distinctions: between intruders and neighbors, between white saviors and people of good will, between racists and the everyday Caucasian citizens trying to get by in an unjust world, just like the rest of us.

Mom didn't sugarcoat anything. She spoke the truth—bluntly, boldly—about how full of shit people could be when it came to Indians. And there are many stories I could share.

But let me be clear: this trauma didn't stem from her being a terrible person or an awful mother, because she wasn't. She's a woman of deep honor, a strong sense of morality, and incredible fortitude. But she was born into poverty and racism handed down by policy and silence.

Her family was once considered wealthy, but they didn't benefit from that wealth. Their land and their money were always controlled by outsiders because they were "Indian." These outsiders did not have their best interests at heart.

Everyone's life includes tragedy and sorrow. It's somehow different when those hardships are systematically inflicted on an entire people, generation after generation. That's not a tragedy—that's an outrage. It's genocide, and it will always remain one of history's darkest marks.

After all that history, it's hard not to turn inward. For me—for now—I've chosen not to retell every trauma I inherited, those stories filled with my mother's fire and fury. I won't speak for her, only offer a brief glimpse into her past.

She has every reason to be proud. She made good decisions. She protected us from the world—maybe too much so. I was a little naïve stepping into adulthood. But isn't that every parent's dilemma? We act from what we know, from the beliefs and survival tools passed down to us.

Still, I see the signs. I see how generational trauma trickled down. And no matter how hard we try to break the cycle, it clings to us–quietly, stubbornly, like dog hair on black, spandex, yoga pants.

My mom married a white man, my dad. He was a wonderful father, a kind, gentle, and expressive person. He could show love and approval easily. She was more guarded. But when you needed someone in your corner—someone to fight for you—you wanted her.

Together, they had a great romance for a marriage. He understood her in a way only true love can.

She had lessons for us about "being Indian." "You don't trust anyone. But especially not a white man." That always confused me because we were part white. Also, Dad, a white man, was amazing. But still, she taught what she knew, which included:

You don't take anything from the government you haven't worked for. That way, the government can't take it back. I don't know if she was consciously referring to the horrors of the Allotment Era. We'll get to that later—but it makes sense. She wasn't talking about income taxes.

She was talking about pride. That mindset gave all her children an incredible work ethic, and as trauma can be passed on, so can good things, because all her children, grandchildren, and great-grandchildren alike have an excellent work ethic.

My other important lesson on "being Indian" is "never let a man disrespect you." She said, "Being an Indian *woman*, a man will **think** he can disrespect you—but you don't let him. Even if you have to knock the shit out of him." And if necessary, I did.

That lesson served me well in my Navy career. Back then, some men believed that if a woman refused to cave to sexual harassment, she shouldn't have enlisted. So, when someone crossed the line—with inappropriate contact or vulgar remarks—I took Mom's advice. I knocked the shit out of them. At one of my commands, it earned me the nickname BamBam.

Eventually, I realized that approach was scaring off the good ones, too. So, I found new ways to handle myself.

Mom's lessons were about survival; she drilled into us to be proud and never let anyone make you ashamed to be Indian. But knowing how to move through the "white man's world"—a world she didn't trust—was different altogether.

Still, I see the signs. I see how generational trauma trickled down. And...I now wonder...how has this affected my children? I fear the cycle is not yet broken. It continues...

GENERATIONAL TRAUMA

I wish I'd known more about the skeletons in my closet while growing up. I wish I'd understood the anger in my mother, the anxiety in myself. I wish I'd known that what I felt wasn't mine alone but part of something passed down, part of something bigger.

Mom did her best to survive in a world that was set against her from the start. Growing up in Tulsa as an Indian, she felt the difference. She lived in a community that devalued Indians, just like we still live in a world that fails to value us.

She grew up in a large family with four sisters and five brothers, so there were ten altogether. Yes, I know you are thinking it— there were *ten little Indians*, and in 1951, they lost their mother to pancreatic cancer. After Louina's death, the two oldest sisters Francis and June raised the rest of the children.

Where was their father you may be wondering? As mom put it...her father ran off with a whore. Wittingly, I say, *"Oh, mother."* ☺ But that is her way— honest, direct, sometimes cutting. She had a gift for storytelling and didn't flinch from the truth.

But before this cold, cruel world left ten little Indians to fend for themselves, a whole set of events were put into place long before this time in 1951. Events that tried to destroy my ancestors. Events that included greed, graft, murder, betrayal, theft, swindle, and so much more. It was a time of chaos and corruption. It was hard to tell who was the good guy, who was the bad guy, and who was just trying to survive!

Six of Louina's children, the Sundays —a moment in time.

There was conflict...

There were tribal conflicts, government conflicts,
The American Civil War.
There were broken treaties, broken promises,
and betrayal we could not ignore.

The progressive leadership said yes,
we must progress, lest we be forgotten.

The traditional leadership saw their world rapidly changing.
Unable to stop the change
they were determined to keep their language and traditions.

They knew to take stock as they were about to face...
culture shock.

Family Tree

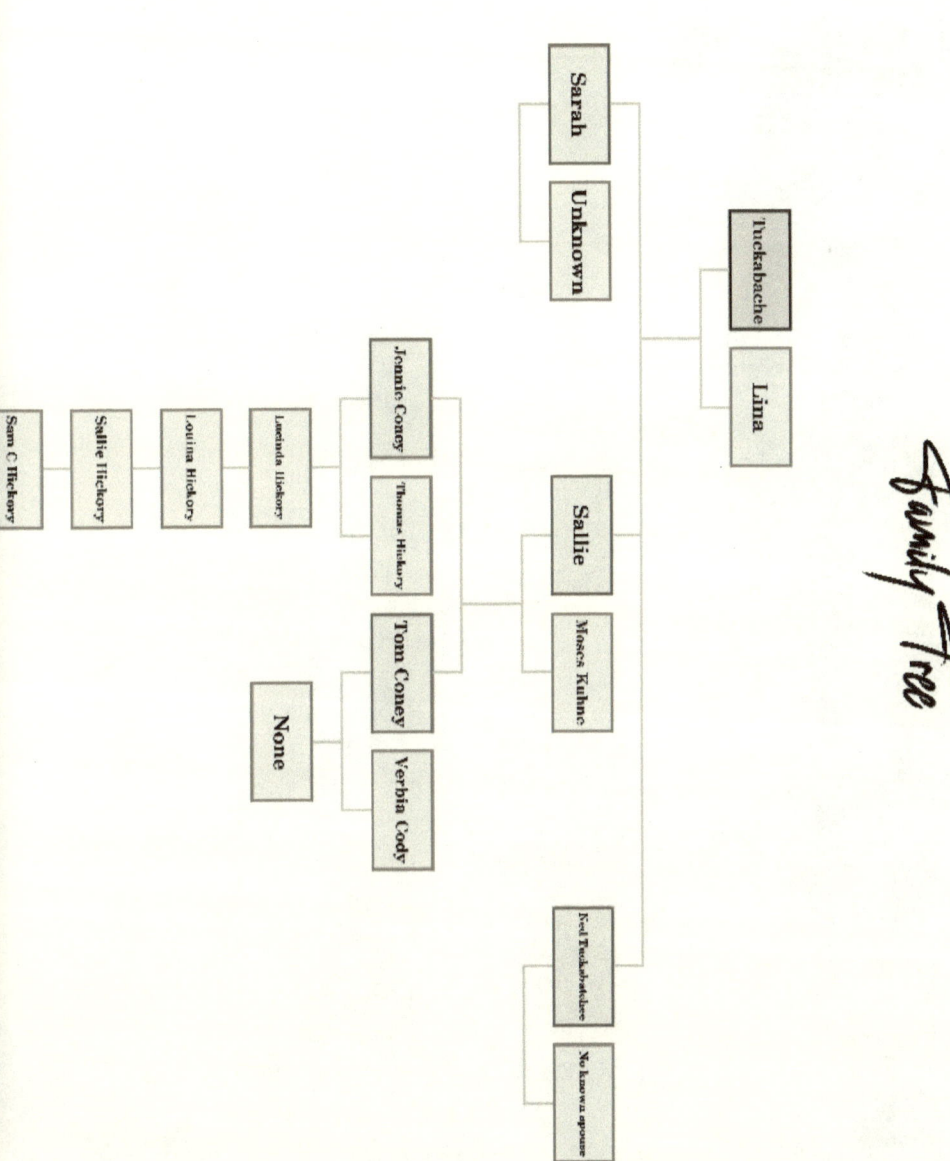

Sarah

Unknown

Tuckabache

Lina

Jennie Coney

Thomas Hickory

Sallie

Moses Kuhne

Lucinda Hickory

Louina Hickory

Sallie Hickory

Sam C Hickory

Tom Coney

Verbia Cody

None

Fed Tuckabatchee

No known spouse

Family Tree

Chapter 2

We Called it Tvlse (Tulsa)

From Great Creek Warrior to the Improvident Indian

I describe the death of Tuckabache as the end of the last generation of great Creek warriors for a very specific reason. We come from warriors like Tuckabache, Chitto Harjo, Opothleyahola, and Isparhecher—leaders who understood that this change would be devastating to Creek culture and to the Creek people. Men who stood alongside them like Redbird of the Cherokees, fought with the full-bloods and traditional Indians to maintain our traditions and language. But for many American Indians, survival meant doing their due diligence to stay a step or two ahead of the grafters. But the grafters knew the game—hell, they invented the game, and they kept changing the rules to ensure they would take all.

The Hickory family...

The children, grandchildren and great-grandchildren of these warriors were left to navigate the system without the guidance of their tribal governments. Forced into assimilation by Indian Boarding schools, separated from their communities, language and traditions. Some placed their trust in the United States government—perhaps out of necessity, perhaps out of hope—but that trust was soon shattered, leaving only mistrust.

The destruction didn't stop at Indian boarding schools; allotment furthered the damage. By the time of Tuckabache's death, his wife Lina and all of his children had already passed. His daughter Sallie, had died just before allotment, leaving behind her husband, Moses Coney (Kuhne, pronounced Cooney), and their two children—Jennie Hickory (née Coney) and Tom Coney, all full-blood Creeks.

Ned died before his father, Tuckabache, leaving behind his own 160-acre allotment which became part of the Tuckabache estate. If you were alive on or after April 1, 1899, you were entitled to receive an allotment — even if you died the next day.

Moses died shortly after his wife, Sallie, leaving behind his 160-acre allotment. With the passing of his parents, Tom Coney, soon found himself under the guardianship of Sam Davis.

Jennie Coney married Thomas Hickory, and together they had four children: Lucinda, Louina, Sallie, and Sammie C. Hickory. Tom Coney went on to marry Verbia Cody but had no children.

The surviving bloodline/heirs of Tuckabache only include his grandchildren: Jennie Hickory, Tom Coney, and his great-grandchildren: Lucinda, Louina, Sallie, and Sammie Hickory. All full-blood Creek Indian.

And what this family was about to face would twist the promise of prosperity into a living hell. The very settlers who came to Indian Territory chasing the American Dream inflicted yet another American Nightmare on Indians who had already been driven from their homelands only seventy years earlier—forced west along Nene Estemerkv, Creek for "The Road of Misery," under the Indian Removal Act.

On a final note, and just to connect the dots of this lineage: Louina Hickory married Cherokee, William Sunday, they had 10 children, one being my mother Sallie Ann Sunday. She married non-Native, Donald Keblish, and together they had four children—one of them being me, Tatianna Keblish Duncan.

The Grifters and the Grafters...

It was not fate that determined their suffering, but the nefarious behavior of dishonest men—some of them the most prominent citizens of Tulsa, men still remembered today. J.M. Hall, often called the founding father of Tulsa. Dr. J.C.W. Bland, considered by some as the city's first doctor. Both celebrated as pioneers of Tulsa.

Along with mayors, city officials, lawyers, and judges alike were deeply complicit in this conspiracy.

Dr. J.C.W. Bland was a key player in the Hickory family affairs, along with his brother-in-law Samuel C. Davis *(half-breed)*, who were instrumental in dispossessing the Hickory family of their estates.

Sam married a white woman, Ethel Davis. We will learn more about his family later in the story.

Dr. J.C.W. Bland and Mrs. Sue Bland...

Dr. Bland's wife, Sue Bland, held one of the first oil-producing allotments in the Tulsa area — Red Fork, the very land that ignited the oil boom soon to engulf Indian Territory.

This was no accident. While Sue and her husband lived on the land, they had not yet filed it as her allotment through the Dawes Commission. Before allotment, men like Fred S. Clinton, Samuel C Davis, Pleasant Porter as well as other educated or "progressive" Creeks were already utilizing Creek land for cattle operations. Men like Dr. JCW Bland were part of that venture. The promise of a 160-acre allotment didn't appeal to them — it threatened their business and their profits.

But what they were about to discover would put them "back in business." The question is, at what cost — and who would pay the price?

One "unsuspecting" day, while Bland and Clinton were walking across this unclaimed property, they noticed a strange liquid seeping from the ground. It looked like oil. Acting quickly, they filled a bottle with the substance and planned to take it to Muskogee, Oklahoma, for testing. But when Bland suddenly suffered an attack of acute appendicitis, Clinton forged ahead—alone.

He obtained a power of attorney from Sue Bland and, in the dark of night, traveled to Muskogee, where he met another doctor friend. Together, they went into the backyard, put a flame to the liquid substance, and watched as it burst into fire — exactly what they were hoping for. They poured it into a kerosene lamp and the lamp burned bright, lighting up the backyard. They celebrated, they knew they had struck oil.

Bland and Clinton remained very close lifelong friends, which makes it hard for me to believe that Dr. Fred S. Clinton was unaware of Bland's darker dealings — the ones we'll uncover later.

As I read The Chronicles of Oklahoma — Clinton's own recollection of these events — I was appalled by his casual disregard for the people whose lives would be devastated by their industrial ventures. Clinton himself, though listed on the Dawes Rolls as one-eighth Creek and holding his own allotment, described life in the area as all there is to do are "a few stomp dances and picnics."

His remarks felt dismissive and condescending. Did these men — Creek or not — ever stop to consider the impact of their actions? Did they care how many Indians and Freedmen they were hurting in their pursuit of success?

I'll leave you with one more story about Bland before we move into why this book had to be written.

Dr. J.C.W. Bland had delivered a paper on pneumonia before the medical society, speaking "intelligently on the matter." Shortly after his wife Sue became ill and on February 18, 1910, she quitclaimed her oil-rich allotment to her seven children. The very next morning, she was dead of pneumonia — shocking Tulsa's elite.

I'm not claiming conspiracy but knowing what I know about the Allotment Era — and about Dr. Bland — the timing is conspicuous. Even the Tulsa County Medical Society felt compelled to issue a resolution, with Dr. Fred S. Clinton remarking that Sue's death was a "strange coincidence."

Could a brother or a husband kill for gain? History and true-crime stories tell us the answer is yes. People do kill loved ones — for land, for money, for control, it seems like for anything.

We will see Bland and Davis appear again and again throughout this story — along with attorney James H. Sykes. For now, pictured below is Dr. Fred S. Clinton.

DR. FRED S. CLINTON.

Dr. Fred S. Clinton, one of Tulsa's earliest physicians and civic leaders, played a pivotal role in the city's early oil boom and public health development.

Photo credit: the Tulsa World, August 31, 1913.

MRS. SUE A BLAND, OF RED FORK, DIES

After a brief illness of five days, Mrs. Sue A. Bland, wife of Dr. J. C. W. Bland, of Red Fork, Okla., died this morning at 6:30 of pneumonia.

Aside from her husband, she leaves one brother, Samuel C. Davis of this city, one sister, Mrs. Minnie Offut of Sapulpa, and seven children, Vera, Era, Owen, Hazel, John C., Arlie and Davis.

Upon the maternal side Mrs. Bland is of distinguished Indian ancestory, her mother being a full-blood Indian. Her father, Mr. Jeff Davis, was a white man, coming to this country originally from Alabama. Mrs. Bland was born in the Choctaw Nation, Indian Territory, about forty-two years ago. She was educated in the National school, and about the year of 1886 was married to Dr. J. C. W. Bland of Red Fork.

The many staunch friends of the family were shocked to learn of Mrs. Bland's death and through various means are expressing their rsympathy to those bereft.

The funeral services will be conducted from the home of her brother, Mr. S. C. Davis, who lives on Fifth and South Boston, in Tulsa.

The Tulsa Tribune
(Tulsa, Oklahoma),
Sat, Feb 19, 1910

The wife of Dr. J. C. W. Bland of Red Fork was said to have died of pneumonia—just weeks after her husband delivered a public address on that very disease. Dr. Fred S. Clinton presided over the medical society's meeting where her death was formally noted, calling it "a strange coincidence."

MRS. BLAND LAID TO REST

Funeral This Afternoon From The Davis Residence in This City.

who died at her home in Red Fork last Saturday, was held from the home of Samuel C. Davis at the corner of Boston and Fifth streets at 1:30 this afternoon. Rev. C. W. Kerr of the First Presbyterian Church officiating.

A large number of the friends of the deceased and the family were present at the funeral and accompanied the remains to Oaklawn cemetery where an impressive ceremony was held prior to interment.

At a meeting last Saturday night the Tulsa County Medical Society passed resolutions on the death of Mrs. Bland.

The president called the meeting to order and Dr. Fred S. Clinton said:

Mr. President: The Grim Reaper has come to the home of one of the members of this society and claimed the companion and wife. Many of you were doubtless surprised or shocked today when you learned of the death of the wife of Doctor J. C. W. Bland. Those of you who attend the Medical Society meetings will recall that he only recently presented a paper upon pneumonia. Consequently it is a strange coincidence that his wife should be a victim of the disease of which he so intelligently talked.

It is but right and proper that we should acknowledge the Sovereignty of the Arbiter of Human Destinies and out of sympath for our brother practitioner and his family, and with due deference to the memory of the departed dead, I move, Mr. President, the adoption of the following resolution:

Be It Resolved by the Tulsa County Medical Society that the usual program be dispensed with, and that this mark of respect and token of our appreciation be transmitted to Doctor Bland and his family, and that a copy of these resolutions be spread upon the minutes of this society and that copy be furnished the press.

The Tulsa Tribune reports the sudden death of Mrs. Sue A. Bland, Sat, Feb 21, 1910

~ 18 ~

Creeks against Creeks?

It is painful to acknowledge, but we must ask: how much were influential Creek citizens themselves involved in this corruption? What did they stand to gain—or fear to lose—from their participation in this devastation? Every culture confronts this struggle. Leaders make sacrifices in the name of what they believe to be the betterment of their people, but at what cost? And when that cost becomes too high, they too must be held accountable—if nowhere else, then in history.

Former Creek Chief Legus Perryman was one such man. It was not simply that he supported progressivism; perhaps he even saw value in it. The problem is that he did little to protect Creek citizens who were being cheated at every turn—and the documents suggest that Legus, along with David Beaver, may have been also responsible. Survival in a changing world is one thing, but when survival comes at the expense of your own people's future, history must call it what it is.

I don't get into the involvement of J.M. Hall or Mayor John H. Simmons, but I believe they were no innocents in the revolution that overturned Creek land and law, conspiring for the Grand Larceny of Tvlse. But here is a short description of their involvement.

On March 10, 1911, Verbia Coney (née Cody) signed a quitclaim deed transferring her interest in both Tom Coney's 160-allotment and Tom's interest in Tuckabache's 160-acre allotment to Tulsa's so-called "founding father," J.M. Hall.

Just one year later, Hall quitclaimed the same land to Ethel Davis. In other words, the land passed straight into the Davis family, linking directly back to Sam Davis. The timing suggests Hall's ownership was never intended to be permanent but rather a legal maneuver, a temporary step in a much larger game. Which is why I call the Allotment Era nothing more than a coconut shell game.

John H. Simmons, who would later serve as Tulsa's mayor (1916–1918), became the administrator of Jennie Hickory's estate in August 1915—although some accounts suggest it may have been the very day she died. What is certain, not long after, his son Hugh Simmons married Marjorie Ethel Irene Davis, daughter of Sam and Ethel Davis. The entanglements between the Simmons and Davis families ran deep.

With that foundation, this story centers on the Hickory family and how, in a single generation, Indians were recast by these grafters from Great Creek Warrior to the 'Improvident Indian' in a town we once called *Tvlse*.

And with that, Tuckabache is where my story begins in Indian Territory.

"If you don't know the story of Tuckabache...
then you don't know the story of Tulsa."

— JD Colbert, Mvskoke/Chickasaw Native

Chapter 3

TUCKABACHE

Last Generation of Great Creek Warriors

Tuckabache is where my story begins in Indian Territory and where Tulsa's hidden truths are revealed.

A distinct figure of Indian Territory, Tuckabache was both a respected warrior and a medicine man. He was a strong presence in history, though few today know of his endeavors. Strong, rooted, and resolute, he stood among the last generation of great Creek warriors. He fought not only to preserve his way of life, but to defend the sovereignty of his people. The papers wrote: "Like the death of Geronimo, the demise of Tuckabache was the passing of one of the famous Indian characters of the Southwest."

TUCKABACHE

Before we get too far into the weeds let me share a story passed down about Tuckabache:

One summer, when a young Cherokee boy named Jess was playing outside near his family's home, he looked up and saw a towering figure riding toward him on horseback.

The man was huge—so large, Jess swore his feet dragged the ground when he came riding up. He wore full Mvskoke regalia, striking in both size and presence.

Jess's father, a U.S. Marshal in Indian Territory, immediately recognized the visitor. "That's Tuckabache," he said—a respected *Mvskoke* Creek man known throughout the region.

But young Jess didn't wait to find out who he was. The moment he saw Tuckabache, he turned and bolted inside, shouting, "An Indian is coming! An Indian is coming!"

He scrambled beneath the kitchen table, terrified.

His father followed him in, puzzled he asked "Jesse—what are you afraid of? You *are* an Indian."

From underneath the dinner table Jess squirmed, "I know, Dad—but I'm not *that kind* of Indian!"

Years later, Jess would come to know more about Tuckabache than anyone else in his time. But on that day, all he saw was the kind of Indian the world had taught him to fear.

Tuckabache lived through generations of betrayal, tribal conflicts, and the American Civil War. He made the treacherous journey of Nene Estemerke, [Muscogee] the Road of Misery—or, as most know it, The Trail of Tears [Cherokee]—only to watch as allotments further encroached on his freedoms and those of the [Muscogee] Creeks. He resisted every intrusion by the white settlers.

As land allotment came around, there were mixed feelings among Creeks. Some wanted progress, and many wanted to stay in the communities that were full of tradition and purpose. But when the question was put to a vote, it was unanimous: the community did not want allotment.

The greed of the settlers and their lack of understanding of a world they did not know brought a magnitude of corruption that ripped the foundation of innocent people. If you grew up in the wake of forced assimilation as I did, then you heard the stories. They were more like whispers, but we heard them loud and clear.

In my research, I soon learned the oral history we had been told growing up of mysterious deaths and stolen land was tragically confirmed with every page I uncovered. The stolen money, land theft, poisoning of Indians, and ruthless guardians were all documented in stark detail. It was difficult to read, page after page, and day after day. Daunting and haunting, it became all too real.

TUCKABACHE

I came to understand that these injustices were not hidden—they were known to the general public at the time—yet nothing tangible was done to stop them. Advocates for the Indians were always outgunned and outnumbered.

Tuckabache was a traditional full-blood Creek Indian. He never spoke a word of English. Why would he? He was witness to the most heinous actions against his people. He experienced the unwelcome changes that were imposed on and suppressed him, his family, and his people. His people...are known as the Muscogee (Creek) Nation. Would he be proud of Indian leadership today?

Regardless, when allotment was forced on Indian Territory, Tuckabache chose an allotment on the land he had called home for the past 65 years. Land where he laid his ancestors to rest—his mother, his brother, his wife, and, tragically, all of his children. He outlived them all, leaving him to bury the people he loved most.

For someone like Tuckabache, who had been scorned too many times to trust the white man, there was no love for them—or for their customs, for that matter. Some believed he hated them outright. I don't know about that, but what I do know is this: he kept his distance. He lived apart from their world, not interested in their ways. He was no threat to their safety. He simply refused to become a part of their world.

I've often wondered about my grandfather's life, especially in his final days, before he was attacked — the moments no record ever captured. Picture this...

...It's 1910, early March, Tuckabache arises. Much of his life has been spent serving and fighting for his community. He enjoys it when he can spend the day hunting with his loyal hounds by his side. Tuckabache was very old, some report that he was 110 years old, and on this morning all so long ago he was enjoying the beautiful March weather. After a long day of hunting and as the temperatures dropped, he headed back to his cabin. Sitting on his front porch with a blanket thrown over his lap, his hounds settling down by his side. As his eyes grew heavy, he found himself lost in thought, his mind wandering back through the years of turmoil and strife that had marked his life and the lives of his people.

Thinking about Alabama, where he was born, he remembered how his family had made the treacherous journey of Nene Estemerke (Road of Misery) a road marred by suffering and loss. I'm sure that carried a resolve in Tuckabache until his death.

Finding himself very alone with everyone moving out of their Tribal Towns to these allotted lands. Tuckabache's heart ached for the Mvskoke way that seemed ever more distant with each passing year.

I'm sure he pondered the division within the tribe, a split deepened by the rise of leaders of mixed heritage who often embraced ideologies and lifestyles far removed from the traditional Mvskoke values. Tuckabache couldn't shake the feeling that these leaders, in their dealings with the government, had not always safeguarded the interests of the full-blood Mvskoke people or their traditions. The relentless push of western expansion had claimed many innocent Indian lives, a fact that seemed of little consequence to those driving it forward.

But I'm so curious about his memories of the unspeakable bond that was present that day...a long time ago, when the tribal town Locv Pokv rekindled their sacred fire in an unfamiliar land, that they would now call home...Indian Territory. The pain they all carried in silence from seeing those they loved suffer in unconceivable ways. That time under the Council Oak Tree was a time of healing, a time to remember, and a time to start anew. His clan, the Snake Clan, came together in ceremony and dance. The complete sense of sanctuary, that day, with his mother and brother standing only steps away. As they were releasing the grief from the trials of this horrific journey.

They would replace pain with peace because it had been missing for so long. Recalling the insurmountable love they all experienced that day, it must have filled his heart with some consolation and comfort, still cradling his spirit as he sat on his front porch, lost in these thoughts. He could feel the warm embrace of his community, at that very moment, from when they were all together, under the Council Oak Tree.

The Council Oak Tree

At the end of the trail, there was a promise,
a promise which we never knew.

At the end of the trail, there was Indian Territory
for us to start anew.

At the end of the trail, in ceremony,
we danced around the sacred fire, as we calmed the pain.

At the end of the trail, this did not last,
as their promise was made in vain.

At the end of the trail there was a mere moment in time
where we replaced the pain for peace.

At the end of the trail, we called this place,
the Council Oak Tree.

Like the death of Geronimo, the demise of Tuckabache was the passing of one of the famous Indian characters of the Southwest.

—Talala Gazette, March 31, 1910

Chapter 4

THE DEATH OF TUCKABACHE

The three White men and the will.

Even today, careless or self-serving historians have wrongfully tarnished his legacy with the charge of slaveholding—a claim that twists absence of evidence into slander. To wrongfully brand a man in death, when he cannot defend himself, is not only unjust but cruel. It is an attack that extends beyond him, striking at his people and his memory. As if the theft of his land were not enough—they would steal his honor too. In my claims, I come armed with evidence to set the record straight, not compete in the politics of victimhood or sensationalism. The truth stands on its own.

Tuckabache rejected white customs; he lived apart from them, not within them. To brand him otherwise is more than a mistake—it is a treachery. It is an attack on a man who endured so much injustice in life. And now even in death, he is not spared from the assaults.

Now let's go back to 1910, to the three white men and the will. Three prominent men of Tulsa—M.F. Smith, Chas Grimes, and John T. Krammer—show up at Tuckabache's cabin with *"full-blood* Creek," David Beaver, to translate the transaction of drafting a will. [i]

M.F. Smith oversaw the affairs of the Creek elder whom he barely knew. Smith is believed to have made deals in Tuckabache's name—deals the elderly man may or may not have known about.

A lot was stirring in the week or two before Tuckabache's death. Marriages were being planned, wills were being drafted, and all eyes were fixed on one man—an old Indian named Tuckabache.

For context: I identify two groups in particular who wanted control over his affairs. The first included three white men and a full-blood Creek named David Beaver, who together drafted a version of Tuckabache's will. The second group involved former Creek Chief Legus Perryman and Sam Davis—though Davis himself wasn't present when Legus visited Tuckabache. Whoever gained the authority to draft the final will held the power to control both the sale of his land and the fate of those who stood to benefit.

Tuckabache had already endured threats. In the days before his death, he was reportedly involved in a physical altercation with grafters who had tried to intimidate him—first by firing pistols into the air, then by force. He fought them off; he was no stranger to battle. But the attack left his eye swollen, dazed, and slipping in and out of consciousness.

Legus Perryman had visited him only a day or two before the white men. He declined to draft a will, saying he did not believe Tuckabache was of sound mind for such a transaction. Yet the men who barely knew him—and who could not speak a word of Creek—decided he was perfectly capable.

Legus had known Tuckabache personally. Though both were full-blood Creek, they were not the same. Legus was more prone to the power of the dollar than the power of community. After all, he had once stood as a witness to the government's forced imposition of a right-of-way easement across Tuckabache's own land.

But it was Legus's deal with the federal government that truly revealed his priorities. Legus was the Chief of the Muscogee (Creek) Nation from 1887-1895, where he upsold the U.S. government while selling out his own people. Creek, Oklahoma, homelands were sold to the U.S. government for thirty cents an acre to be used for Indian purposes only. [ii]

In his biography, Legus boasts that in 1886, he introduced selling land intended for Indian purpose only, for an extra ninety-five cents an acre and planned to open it up to white settlement. When he became Chief in 1887, he finalized this deal. [iii] This act utterly contrasted with the values of Tuckabache and other Creeks like the staunch Creek advocate Chitto Harjo, who resisted the government's allotment policies to his dying breath.

Still, they had been through a lot together—tribal conflicts, and the American Civil War among them—and they witnessed many of the same changes. Although they had different visions for the future of Creek Nation, Tuckabache being traditional and Legus more progressive, they still knew each other well.

Whether they were truly friends or merely comrades, they shared a long history. Legus, fluent in both Creek and English, would seem like a natural choice to draft Tuckabache's last will alongside David Beaver. They seemed like likely allies. But there were many forces at play. With Legus involved in land and real estate dealings alongside his friend and business partner, Samuel C. Davis, it's possible this was more about competition between speculators vying for control rather than protecting a lifelong friendship.

Samuel C. Davis being half Creek and half white was a trusted figure in the community. He was considered a friend by many Creeks, including the grandchildren of Tuckabache, the Hickorys. That trust— once given freely—would come at a devastating cost. Many Indians were left vulnerable, and men like Sam Davis knew it.

Speaking about the actions of Sam Davis, we know who was there in the broad of daylight drafting wills, but who was there the night Tuckabache was assaulted at his cabin? At this point in 1910, the grifters and the grafters were bold and brutal. It seemed to be all or nothing for them.

Tuckabache confided in Legus that some fellow had been abusing him. It was one of the last conversations Tuckabache had with Legus or perhaps with anyone, for that matter. In Tuckabache's probate hearing, the courts asked Legus about their last conversations, and he was hesitant to share this information.

"I don't know whether I ought to say," he replied. "It is immaterial and kind of a family affair." Legus continued, "he said that some fellow had been abusing him."

When pressed on who it was, Legus remained evasive, saying only that Tuckabache had "intimated" at someone but hadn't named them outright. Then Legus added, "He went to a pretty big random place, and he said someone went there and disturbed him by shooting off a pistol or aiming to shoot a pistol." [iv]

Finally, when the court asked directly if he knew who it was, Legus admitted, "I knew who it was," but Legus never did say.

Why wouldn't Legus name the man? Why did the court not insist on an answer? With his business ties to Sam Davis, a man whose influence seemed to shadow many such suspicious affairs, one wonders if Legus was holding something back, intentionally or otherwise.

Tuckabache's death is becoming more and more evident that it was not of natural causes. Within

Tuckabache's final financial records of the administrator, M.F. Smith, were some odd purchases, such as chloroform, syringes, and "carbolic acid." This discovery was a hair-raising experience, a document that had been in my possession for a couple of years before I actually realized its existence.

I had no idea at the time what carbolic acid was, but it didn't sound very nice. I learned it was commonly used as a sanitizer such as a household cleaner, but darker uses also emerged...suicides and murders... and so goes the allotment era.

Tuckabache was old, and he had lived! I consider myself a strong person, but I wonder, could I have survived like he did and like his great-granddaughter, Louina? They were remarkable in their environment. They fought back and stood up to the corruption surrounding them, but sadly, this was not enough.

It was said that Tuckabache had the most beautiful and pristine land in all of Oklahoma. Today, it is a park called Gathering Place. Land-grafters had an eye on his property and approached him many times to buy it. Tuckabache turned a deaf ear to them every time. The grafters never stopped their pursuit of his land. If he'd had his way, Tuckabache would have lived the rest of his life without another white man imposing his ways. But once Indian land was divided into individual allotments, the conspiracy to take it began. And that's where the Midland Valley Railroad comes in. The tracks ran right through his property, whether he wanted them to or not.

Tuckabache fought the railroad the best he could, resisting the encroachment of white industry and their "progress," but it was a losing battle.

The railroad was coming—its plans laid long before allotment. One old Indian, two old Indians, even a resistance of many Creek men like Chitto Harjo and the Crazy Snake Rebellion couldn't stop the toxic machine they called "progress."

The grafters and speculators were relentless in their desire to acquire the land he lived on for sixty-five years. His family was buried there. It was home. To them, Tuckabache, a well-respected elder, was just an obstacle standing in the way of their profit.

And as if the railroad wasn't enough of an intrusion, there was always more. A settler claimed a verbal contract to lease a portion of Tuckabache's property for two years. Ownership itself was a new and foreign concept for Creeks like Tuckabache, who came from a culture of caring for one another and sharing resources. If someone needed land to stay on, would he have said no? Possibly not. But once he saw how the land was being treated, he protested. The settler failed to cultivate it properly, and Tuckabache wanted him gone.

I suspect that a lot of these transactions were without Tuckabache's full knowledge, Smith leased out the land and defended the settler's presence. The courts sided with Smith, not with Tuckabache. It leaves me wondering: were they simply dismissing his wishes, or were they already poking around for minerals, or planning a neighborhood, positioning themselves for his demise, and preparing to build on land that wasn't theirs? It was after all believed Tuckabache was over 100 years old.

The disagreement over the land escalated into a legal battle, one of the many that Tuckabache's family would face in the years to come. In court, the judge ruled against Tuckabache, claiming the old Indian had made a deal and needed to live up to his word. Did he, though?

Did Tuckabache truly agree to this? Full blood Creek, non-English speaking Tuckabache? Or was it just another deal orchestrated by M.F. Smith, who saw his own interests as more legitimate than those of the land's rightful owner? And what right did the judge have to speak of broken promises when treaties and agreements with the Creek people had been consistently shattered by greed?

The hypocrisy is almost too much to bear, a justice system built on principles it had no intention of upholding. And what was about to unfold in Tulsa would make the mere eviction of a tenant seem trivial in comparison.

The truth is, outsiders like M.F. Smith were always looking for ways to create revenue from land that was only theirs to covet. Leasing out Tuckabache's land, working deals behind his back, this was the foundation of all the evil that defined this era. The legal system in Indian Territory was never built to protect American Indian landowners. It was created to facilitate the transfer of land to white hands, whether through forced sales, guardianships, or fraudulent deals like this one.

Men like Smith had connections; they had power. They knew the courts would always side with them, and no matter how much Tuckabache fought, the system would find a way to take what was his.

In Tuckabache's case, the legal battle over his land, the leases made with or without his consent, and the court's insistence that he "live up to his word" were just some of the deeds that led to a state of corruption.

I found it odd how I had, for all my life growing up, heard that Indians had been poisoned. I was surprised to learn that this was not common knowledge. But when I learned of Tuckabache's death, I did not give it another thought. He was an old man. Lived longer than most. No doubt a survivor of some deadliest times in history, but everyone will have their day when the journey here is over. But we prefer that it is a natural process, not at the hands of the nefarious behavior of dishonest men.

What I once considered an endearing sentiment that warmed my heart, as I felt I had found a connection with my third great grandfather. A news article wrote that he requested that he be buried with his gun, knife, and other implements of the chase... When I first read this article, I thought of the spirit of a warrior. If we could dig up Tuckabache and retrieve those implements of the chase, how amazing that would be! To hold in my hands what he once held in his...

...And as those thoughts were racing through my mind, I continued to read he had requested that salt be sprinkled in his grave to detour marauders from disinterring it.

I felt immediate embarrassment at my thoughts, yet an appreciation that I had learned something substantial from the grave of my grandfather.

Did I, though? As time went on, so did my research, and with every discovery, my understanding of Tuckabache's life—and death—began to change. What I once found endearing now raises more questions than answers. His death no longer seemed like the peaceful passing of an old man. The red flags were everywhere. And suddenly, I had to rethink everything. What about the request to sprinkle salt in his grave? Was that really a tradition... or part of a cover-up?

Three days after the "three white men" drafted a will for Tuckabache, he was dead— and buried the very next morning.

Today, I'm not just connected to Tuckabache by blood. I'm connected by a glimpse into his life. The deeper I dug, the more certain I've become that my third great-grandfather, Tuckabache, did not die of natural causes...he was murdered.

TUCKABACHE IS DEAD.

Died Aged 110 Years—He Hated the Whites.

The body of Tuckaba...
oldest medicine...
Creek nati...

Foe of White Men Dies.

Tulsa, Okla., March 21. — At the age of 101, Tuckabache, a noted full-blood Creek Indian chief, died upon his allotment, six miles south of this city. He had been ill but a few days.

TUCKABACHE WAS HATER OF WHITES

Like the death of Geronimo, the demise of Tuckabache was the passing of one of the famous Indian characters of the Southwest.

MEDICINE MAN GONE

Tuckabache, oldest Indian known, gone to Happy Hunting Ground.

BORN IN THE YEAR 1800

, said to be the oldest e state, died at his

INDIAN HOLDS FORT.

Old Tuchabache Will Not Part With His Land.

SAPULPA, Okla., August ?
mood and with silent
white brother, T...
dian more ...

DEATH CLAIMS TUCKABACHE

WAS ONE HUNDRED AND TEN YEARS OLD.

...ME HERE IN 1834

Oldest Indian a Defendant.

Tuckabache, the oldest living Indian in the Creek nation, at the age of 105, in Justice Gilliland's...

A Noted Creek Indian Dead.
At the age of 101, Tuckabache, a noted full-blood Creek Indian chief, died upon his allotment six miles south of Tulsa yesterday. He had been ill but a few days. Like Crazy Snake, Tuckabache was a Creek In-dis-

Newspapers fixated on his resistance to white settlement, framing him as a "hater" rather than a man defending his land and people. The language itself tells the story of how history was written — and by whom.

CONTRA

.................asks to be credited with the following sums, paid out as per receipts exhibited.

DATE			ITEMS PAID OUT.	AMOUNT		TOTAL AMT.	
Month	Day	Year		Dolls.	Cts.	Dolls.	Cts.
May 25		1910	Notary Fees		50		
	26		Axle grease		10		
	26		Chloroform		30		
	26		Carbolic acid		10		
Aug	3		Joe Tiger for fixing fence		60		
	3		Three cow yokes	2	25		
	22		Wire and staples	2	75		
Sept	2		Joe Tiger foxing fence		30		
	2		Burnt alum		10		
	22		Railroad fare		94		
Oct	5		Chloroform and syringe		85		
Nov	4		Joe Tiger fixing fence	2	85		
	10		Paid Foster for hauling corn	9	36		
Dec	9		Paid Holt for crying sale	2	00		
Dec 10			Joe Tiger for work	5	10		
Dec 10			Black Printing Co for printing sale bills	1	50		
		1911					
Mar	1		Wire and staples	2	75		
	3		Copy of will	1	25		
	17		Crews & Carter--Lumber	5	65		
Apr 29			Advertising pasture		45		
May 23			Digging on well	3	00		
Feb 18			John J. Slack Court Costs	3	00		
Mar 24			S. Edy-Lock and chain		40		
			Total-------------------	$ 46	10		

1913 Nov. By Amt. paid Ewing Adv. Co.   5.25

$51.35

Expenses recorded by a guardian,
M. F. Smith in 1910–1911, including
purchases of chloroform, syringes,
carbolic acid, and other items.

Land Ownership

*The US government wanted land ownership for the Indians.
But the Elders said, "No! That is not our way."*

*The US government said, "But that is the only way you will be
civilized, that is the only way you will survive."*

*The Elders knew that was wrong and said,
"No... You do not understand.*

*Our people are not ready for citizenship;
they are not ready for the change.*

*Our people do not speak the language;
you do not understand.*

Our people do not believe that man should own the land."

Remembering Tuckabache

If it's true that Tuckabache once asked for salt to be sprinkled in his grave so grave robbers would leave him in peace, then what happened in 1921 was more than a violation — it was an outrage. They dug up his entire family's burial ground at Cincinnati and Harvard to make way for their mansions. Land that, by law, should not have been sold for 25 years —desecrated— removing those who had been laid to rest.

Tuckabache's name has lingered through the years as an extraordinary figure in our history, yet most cannot say why. I believe that silence comes from two things: the language stolen from my elders through forced assimilation, and the flaw in how history is recorded. Those who thrived in the colonized world were remembered; those who resisted it were not. Their absence isn't because the colonizers were victors — it's because they were deceivers. And there is no honor in that.

The record books celebrate the Perrymans, a "diverse" Indian family who embraced progressivism. They honor Alexander Posey; a Creek poet educated in the colonized ways. They elevate Thomas Gilcrease — who claimed Creek heritage but lived far from the Indian world. And, as for the Creek stories I've heard, was no ally to his Creek neighbors. Ask his descendants, and you may hear another version of his legacy.

Your family story matters. If you can't find your ancestors celebrated in the history books, it's not because they didn't contribute. It's because they stood for something different, for keeping their Native ways — and history didn't find that worth remembering.

In death, the irony lingers. Dr. Bland now lies in the same cemetery as Tuckabache — perched about 150 hundred yards away, elevated on an incline, as if still overlooking him and the Hickory family. It feels as though they can never escape his shadow.

Even with all that said, Tuckabache—now buried at Oaklawn Cemetery—lies beneath a massive cement monument engraved in the language he did not speak. Above his head lies the unseen—a mass grave containing many of his relatives, their remains abruptly taken from their resting place at Cincinnati and Harvard and unceremoniously thrown into a pit above his headstone. The words carved to describe him do not hold the truth of his life. Yet there his bones must rest, the world never knowing the fullness of his Este Cate (Indian) life.

Chapter 5

THE PROBATE BATTLE

The coconut shell game begins!

Now, here comes Sam & Ethel Davis, moving quickly on the Hickory family, the heirs of Tuckabache, to take control of the Tuckabache estate. Unfortunately for the Davis's, there was that pesky will devised by the three white men. And with that, the probate battle was on.

There was much debate over the validity of Tuckabache's will though the circumstances surrounding it were questionable from the start. When it was first contested, the judge ruled it invalid. Still, that initial ruling wasn't the end of it. The only person who could testify that Tuckabache had agreed to the will was David Beaver, a full-blood Creek, as none of the other men present spoke Creek, and Tuckabache didn't speak

English. David, being the only one who spoke both Creek and English, served as the sole witness. However, the judge noted that two witnesses were required for the will to be valid. But, as expected, Smith appealed, and the grafters didn't stop until they got the decision that they schemed for—the will was eventually declared valid.

With grafters in place such as Smith, Bland, and Davis, the odds were stacked against "full-blood Creeks." And whether the will was valid or not, and whether it was Sam Davis, the man who initially contested the will, or the three white men who ultimately prevailed, I am sure of one thing: it didn't matter! The family was never going to benefit from their inheritance. The system was rigged, and men like Davis and Bland were deeply entrenched in that corruption.

Samuel C. Davis, or Sam Davis, was no stranger to the Creek people. In fact, he was half Creek and once served as the private secretary for Chief Legus Perryman. The Creeks trusted him, and as a wheeler and dealer, Sam Davis knew exactly how to manipulate the system to enrich himself, and he had no qualms about cheating the Creek people who trusted him out of their land and wealth. He may have had Creek blood, but he was no ally to his tribe. He was tethered to the white world of power and profit, Tulsa's high society.

Back to the three white men who visited Tuckabache while he was on his deathbed. Attorney Chas Grimes, despite his lack of experience as a drafter of wills, was charged with the responsibility of writing the will. Then there was the Tulsa County treasurer, John T. Kramer who said he had "been to see Tuckabache several times," yet also admitted he had no dealings with Tuckabache and could not speak his language. His testimony contradicts itself — raising the question of why he was there at all.

Why did Grimes and Smith call upon the Tulsa County treasurer to witness a will for a man none of them truly knew? Smith made decisions on Tuckabache's behalf despite not speaking his language, and Tuckabache was known to mistrust white men and their customs. These facts don't align.

M.F. Smith, who had been managing Tuckabache's affairs, was leading the charge. Together, these men were not friends of Tuckabache; they barely knew him. They did not understand him. Not his language or his customs.

With more digging, Grimes's motives become clearer: He would benefit greatly from this arrangement. The will set aside 40 acres for, a Creek woman who had been keeping house for Tuckabache, her name, Martha Sevier. However, this too was a ruse because that land would later be quitclaimed to Charles Grimes. He ensured that he wrote himself into this will by making deals with Indians like Martha.

Charles Grimes, the namesake of Grimes Elementary School in Tulsa, not only drafted Tuckabache's last will but also set himself up to profit from the outcome. He purchased some of the land as his law firm collected $400.00 in attorney fees from each of the three Hickory heirs, payments that would total about $30,000 in today's money.

THE PROBATE BATTLE

By June 27, 1917, most of the Tuckabache estate had been taken out of the hands of the Hickory heirs and sold off to Grimes and other land grabbers. Their battles were far from over. The fight over the will had passed, but the overall battle, the battle for the home—was just beginning.

But before we go there, first let me introduce you to Tuckabache's grandson, Samoche, known as Tom Coney (Kuhne-Cooney).

The Swindle...

The Indian Rights Association called
this time in history "legalized theft."
Where the guardians were ruthless to their wards,
and judges turned a blind eye for a buck.

The Oklahoma Supreme Court would agree
with the Indians as they decried,
you cannot sell the restricted land of the Indian,
of the Indian now demised.
You must consider the heritage, the heritage of the Indian,
You must consider the Indian, the Indian who has declared,
If you sell our land, we will be in despair.

But all this fell on deaf ears as real estate developers and
guardians plotted and planned,
until they had the dead Indian's land.

So, you see, if you dig deep enough, you too will soon know...
that the "legalized theft"–was not legal at all.

Chapter 6

THE DANGER OF BEING INDIAN DURING ALLOTMENT:

Name: Tom Coney
Cause of death: Fever
Type: Unknown

Both of Tom Coney's parents, Moses and Sallie Kuhne, had passed away by 1900, leaving him under the guardianship of Sam Davis. His mother, Sallie (Kuhne/Coney) was Tuckabache's daughter, and Moses was her husband.

Little is known about Tom's upbringing, but it's likely he spoke English and was, for half of his life, under the tight control of his guardian, Samuel C. Davis. Tom's allotment bordered his father, Moses Coney's land, to the east and Tuckabache's land to the north. Tom and his grandfather Tuckabache each held a full 160-acre section, while Moses's land was divided into separate locations. Moses's and Tuckabache's son, Ned, both had partial allotments that stretched alongside the Arkansas River—land that today is part of Tulsa's Gathering Place Park. It's one of the many connections to the family's legacy that lives on in the city's modern landscape, though with little recognition of its history.

As Tuckabache lay sick and dying, it wasn't compassion that was by his side. It was ambition! A greedy, dirty ambition that lacked love and concern. Heavy hearted I must realize that these were the final days of my third great-grandfather, Tuckabache, and my great, great Uncle Tom Coney. They were not surrounded by loved ones; they were surrounded by swindlers.

The "red flags" are flying high on this one because it is highly unlikely that while Tuckabache was on his deathbed, Tom would have voluntarily distanced himself from his dying grandfather at such a critical time to marry a "white women." Oral histories passed down in our family warn of the dangers that came with such unions; many Indians lost their lives after marrying into white families during this period.

- March 14, 1910, Tom is marrying Verbia.
- March 18, 1910, a will is being drafted for Tuckabache by three men who barely knew him.
- March 21, 1910, Tuckabache is dead and buried the next morning.
- November 23, 1910 Tom Coney is dead.

In reviewing Tuckabache's final account record, one detail stands out: the plan for Tom Coney's marriage appears less like a union and more like a calculated set for a land grab. The timing is chilling.

In May 1910, the record show purchases of carbolic acid and chloroform. In October, more chloroform and a syringe. By November 23, Tom Coney was dead. Cause of death: "a fever." Type of fever — unknown.

Taken together, these entries raise questions that history has never answered. The financial records tell a quiet story — one of timing, chemicals, and coincidence. Maybe it's nothing. But maybe it's the trace of another young Indian life gone too soon — another silence, history refuses to question.

Tom's older sister, Jennie Hickory (nee` Coney), was interrogated on the same day about his death, particularly concerning her status as his heir. When asked how her brother died, Jennie responded that it was from a fever, though she wasn't sure what kind of fever. This raises further suspicion about Tom's death, especially given the known symptoms of carbolic acid poisoning.

Many of these symptoms align eerily well with what might have been considered a "fever" at the time. Given that carbolic acid poisoning causes severe abdominal pain, vomiting, and fever-like conditions, it's easy to see how the true cause of Tom's death could have gone unrecognized, and perhaps dismissed as a common illness when, in reality, something far more sinister was at play.

Tom Coney died at Tulsa General Hospital on November 23, 1910, just eight months after his marriage to Verbia and eight months after Tuckabache's death. He was 20 years old.

To date, I have found no detailed records of Indian deaths from this period, making it even harder to fully understand the circumstances surrounding Tom's passing—as well as the many other untimely deaths of Native people. One 1905 newspaper article observed, "when it is only a dead Indian, the news is received with a shrug."

After Tom's death, his land became a prime target for land grabbers. Sam Davis, as he had done before, maneuvered to take control of the Hickory family's land. Armed with general warranty deeds, he arranged for Jennie Hickory's interest in the land to be transferred to his wife, Ethel Davis.

Pictured is James H. Sykes, we will talk about him next. Also pictured is Dr. JCW Bland.

Vinita Daily Chieftain
(Vinita, OK), July 23, 1912.

Tulsa Star (Tulsa, OK),
February 20, 1915

VINITA, OKLAHOMA, TUESDAY, JULY 23, 1912.

JAMES H. SYKES
Democratic Candidate Candidate for Congressman, From
Third District of Oklahoma.

James H. Sykes, attorney and politician, later Oklahoma Representative for Tulsa County. His conflicts of interest in Creek guardianship cases and open racist views cast a shadow over his role in Hickory family affairs. — another red flag in a system built on corruption.

Preacher Against Negroes.

Representative Morgan, a Democratic minister of the gospel, made a bitter speech against the Negro:

"They don't need educating," declared Morgan, "for I have observed that the Negro woman takes in washing to support her worthless educated husband. We should take care of the Negro only as far as we are able. This is a white man's country."

Representative James H. Sykes of Tulsa declared that while he was in favor of abolishing every secondary agricultural shool in the state, including the Negro school at Langston, he was in favor of the appropriation at this time.

"The school at Langston," said Sykes, "educates the Negro for agricultural pursuits. The town nigger is a curse and the country nigger is a necessity. I want to see them taught to be useful on the farms and as servants."

Would Put Them in Pen.

Representative Asa E. Walden of Love county quoted poetry in support of his contention that the Negro "had nothing coming to him." "The common schools are good enough for the niggers," he said, "but the best school for them is over at McAlester—the state penitentiary."

"I am in favor of civilizing and Christianizing the Negro," said Representative Wash Hudson of Tulsa, "and if we vote down this bill it will be a curse and a crime."

THE DANGER OF BEING INDIAN DURING ALLOTMENT:

Tulsa Tribune (Tulsa, OK),
January 3, 1928, p. 1.

DR. J. C. W. BLAND

Dr. Bland's Death Recalls By-Gone Days

First Medical School Graduate in Tulsa Dies After Severe Illness

Helped Build an Empire

With Dr. Clinton Made First Discovery of Oil Near Here

When the Frisco railroad stopped at Red Fork, Tulsa's Main street was the avenue of log cabins; the town pump was a matter of consequence, and the country doctor was king—that is where those who know begin the story of the man who died Monday afternoon.

He was Dr. John Charles Willard Bland, 68, of 411 S. Victor av., for 43 years a practicing physician in Tulsa, part owner of the first oil well ever drilled in this section, oldest of this city's pioneer doctors, one of Tulsa's first druggists, cattleman, ranchers, real estate dealers, and civic leaders.

After a severe illness lasting two months Doctor Bland died of stomach and intestinal troubles, while a few friends and relatives stood by. His death had been expected. The body is being held at the Mowbray Undertaking Co.'s mortuary. Funeral services are to be Thursday morning at 11 at the First Presbyterian church. Dr. C. W. Kerr will preach the funeral sermon. Masons will be in charge at the grave. The body will lie in state at the Mowbray Undertaking Co. until the funeral.

HIS STORY IS TULSA'S

The story of Doctor Bland is a story of Tulsa, of oil, of lives—lives that he brought into the world as a pill-and-saddlebag "country doctor."

In 1885—J. M. Hall, the storekeeper, was here then — Doctor Bland rode into Tulsa on a horse.

He was young and fresh from the Missouri Medical school — now Washington university—at St. Louis. Tulsa's first medical school graduate. He had come over from Stillwater, Ok, in search of a location and to Stillwater from Iowa, and Centerville, his birthplace.

Oklahoma, an empire awakening; Tulsa, embryo of that city to become the oil capital of the world; Doctor Bland, a country doctor, to help speed that day when black gold would flow from the earth to bring half a country out of a wilderness. And history received an impetus when Doctor Bland came to Oklahoma and Tulsa.

OPENED DRUG STORE

Near where the Security building now stands at Second and Main streets, Doctor Bland, following his marriage to Miss Sue Arlie Davis, a Tulsa girl, opened one of the city's first drug stores.

From this little pill-and-powder emporium, the doctor's family home being connected with the store, Doctor Bland began many of the trips that led him to probably every doorstep in the then sparsely settled community about Tulsa and Red Fork.

In those days, 40 years ago, log cabins graced dusty Main street. Doctor Bland and his sister-in-law, Mrs. Minnie Offutt, owned the entire block of ground between Boston and Main and Third and Fourth streets, and upon which some of Tulsa's tallest buildings now stand. Doctor Bland sold his share of the property for $1,200. Today—millions would not buy that block.

WAS ALWAYS ACTIVE

For over a quarter of a century and until his illness recently, the physician was a member of the governmental board of pensions and in his early years, served as a member of the first board of medical examiners, and as surgeon for the Mid-

Turn to Page 14, Column 5, Please.

Obituary of Dr. J.C.W. Bland, Tulsa World. Bland is remembered as a "pioneer," alongside men like J.M. Hall and John H. Simmons — names celebrated in Tulsa's history. Yet behind the praise were red flags: attorneys, doctors, businessmen, and land men whose dealings often left Creek families stripped of their land and wealth.

James H. Sykes isn't remembered in Oklahoma history like some of the other names — at least, not that I have found. Maybe that's because of his openly racist views at the time. Even in the days of Jim Crow, people may have preferred less of his candor.

In 1914, Sykes was elected as a Representative for Tulsa County, serving in 1915. His Democratic Party stood on a so-called Friends of the Indian platform, saying Indians were being cheated and needed protection. On the surface it looked like he was on their side. But wasn't he one of the very men cheating the Indians? The answer is yes. In truth, he was setting up a system that worked in his favor. He lobbied to put Indian affairs under the control of the local courts — courts he was already in cahoots with, along with attorneys, guardians, and judges. By forcing everything to go through those courts, he made sure the whole process flowed through people he could influence. It wasn't protection. It was swindle. A mastermind conspiracy — and Sykes was one of the perpetrators.

Sykes was also deeply tied into the Hickory family affairs. The children's guardian, Bland, kept retainers in their name, always tied to their estates. But when the Hickory family themselves needed legal help, usually to sue their guardian, they went outside of Sykes, taking their chance with other local attorneys. Still, their guardian, Dr. J.C.W. Bland, would bring in Sykes — and charge his fees to the children's estates. That meant the Hickory family was trapped in a crooked system: they had to pay for their own attorney, while also footing the bill for their guardian's attorney, as Sykes and Bland, worked hand in hand against them.

Let's do a quick recap, members of Tuckabache's family who received allotments but, by 1910, of those I researched, are no longer living include Moses Coney, Ned Tuckabacthee, Tuckabache, and Tom Coney.

While my story isn't solely about land loss and wealth, its purpose centers on the loss of culture and the treatment of my ancestors. However, the land and wealth provide a tangible measure of the scale of injustice. In all, 640 acres of family land and well over $1,500,000.00 in today's value were lost over a short period.

As for Ned Tuckabatchie's allotment, when Tuckabache's son passed in 1900, it became part of the Tuckabache estate and fell under the larger probate proceedings that governed Tuckabache's land.

But we're not done yet.

We've just begun!

This rocking chair, said to have been built by Dr. J.C.W. Bland and given to my great aunt, Sallie Hickory Sunday, sits in my living room today. Its presence is unsettling. Is it a gift, or a reminder of the complicated, even twisted, ties between the Hickory family and the men who controlled their lives? Of all the land and wealth Bland managed — land that once belonged to the Hickory family — this is what remains. A so-called gift. The irony is not lost on me. The chair, now professionally reupholstered, is it a relic of betrayal or a testament to survival? Maybe both.

The Guardian

The Indian did not know the language;
the Indian was on his own.
The Indian being uncertain, sought to trust someone.

Lurking in the background, just to be their friend,
waiting ever so patiently, we find the greedy guardian.

The guardian called me his friend.
He said I could trust him; he pretended to care.
He said he would help me,
as he told me to put my thumbprint right there.

He dispossessed me of my land.
He tried to dispossess me of everything that I am.
He was not my friend; he was simply my greedy guardian!

Chapter 7

FOREVER YOUNG – LUCINDA

Gone too soon.

Let's jump to 1912 and see if things fare any better. Spoiler alert: they don't. Tuckabache's estate is still tangled in probate, by this time, the Davis family has already illegally gained controlling interest over the Hickory heirs' inheritance. This was their plan: whenever an Indian died, they'd swoop in, collecting deeds, thumbprints, and Xs, to take.

When I say their plan, it wasn't just Sam and Ethel Davis. It was a "state of corruption," the grifters, the grafters, the land and oil speculators, attorneys, and judges. They were all in on it, and those who were not in on it knew about it.

Many knew that collecting thumbprints and X's would enable them to grab land deeds, which turned into land, leverage, and legacy. They were building an economic empire by robbing Indians of what belonged to them.

Lucinda Hickory was only 12 years old when such a theft occurred. Her land tested for 20 millions [cubic feet] in gas. This was her ticket to secure a grand future for herself in a world that was rapidly changing around her. It would allow her to afford the finest education, live comfortably, marry well and raise a strong family. Or, at the very least, a foundation on which to build a future.

She was the eldest of four children and a great-granddaughter of Tuckabache, named as one of the beneficiaries on his "alleged will." She received a 160-acre allotment located at 21st & Harvard in Tulsa, Oklahoma. And when Chief Pleasant Porter signed her allotment deed over to her, what he did not know—he signed her death warrant. Having been sick a few days with "fever," Lucinda died January 3, 1913, eight months after the *Tulsa World* ran this article in their paper:

OIL NEWS AND COMMENT
By W. H. Peck

Oil company (Abby Richards), on the north line of the Grant Smoke farm, as it will determine whether or not there is a trend toward the northeast. It will be remembered that the Oklahoma State Oil company drilled a dry hole on the south end of the Grant Smoke, which was a great surprise to everyone.

The Galbreath test on the Lucinda Hickory in the northwest of section 16-19-13, southeast of Kendall college, is completed and is good for twenty millions of gas. It would appear that there is quite a gas field over there which is worth, of course, lots of money to the city of Tulsa, being right at her door.

be drilled deeper.

In the south end the Prairie Oil & Gas company No. 1 test on the Kennedy farm in section 31-11-13, is an 150-barrel well, while the Advance Oil company No. 5 in the same section is good for only 45 barrels.

The Eastern Oil company did not complete any 2500-barrel well, as rumor had it, in section 18-14-13, but is spudding in tapped a 4-inch line (the Gulf line from Bald Hill), which gave the boys here a chance to hang it on to this old man as a joke. In reality it was the Martin well on the Jackson Pidgeon, which showed so big. It is an offset (same section) to the Eastern Oil company and is good for 400

April 27, 1912,
The Tulsa World reported,

"The Galbreath test on the Lucinda Hickory in the northwest of section 16-19-13, southeast of Kendall College, is completed and is good for twenty millions of gas [*cubic feet of gas.*] It appears there is quite a gas field over there, which is worth, of course, lots of money to the city of Tulsa, being right at her door."

This is where the real problem lies. If it hasn't become clear yet, I'm talking about a culture of people who were thrown into poverty by these events and who today continue to grow up in poverty if they survived at all.

Our community is grappling with the intersection of cultural deprivation, educational disadvantage, and ongoing socioeconomic challenges that persist across generations.

But let's not buy into the myth that American Indians couldn't survive because they were somehow not smart enough or too drunk to manage their own affairs. Every opportunity placed before them was rapidly snatched away.

Dr. W. A. Cook, guardian of Lucinda Hickory, was quietly accumulating wealth from coal production on her land. According to her parents, neither Lucinda nor the family ever saw a dime. When her father, Thomas Hickory, asked about the land's earnings, Cook refused to disclose the amount and refused to share the proceeds. [v]

According to Jennie and Thomas, when the courts asked about the money from Lucinda's land, they replied plainly: "We don't get that—the guardian does."

That reply was evidence. Their daughter's wealth had been stolen by the very man assigned to protect it, and no one in the courtroom seemed concerned or surprised.

Grief hadn't even settled in, and already the paperwork was done. For Jennie and Thomas, it was their daughter's death. For Sam and Ethel Davis, it was just another transaction to line their pockets. Thomas and Jennie Hickory were still coming to terms with their daughter's death, but Sam Davis wasted no time. He filed general warranty deeds at the Tulsa County Courthouse the very day Lucinda died transferring her mineral-rich land into his wife Ethel's name.

We do see in the competency hearing of the Hickorys that they both said they did not sign (X and thumbprint) any deeds until about a week or so later, not the same day.

1b   98.

47295

Thomas Hickory, heir at
law of Lucinda Hickory

–TO–

Ethel Davis

WARRANTY DEED
Dated: January 9, 1913
Filed: Jan. 9, 1913 at 5:00 P.M.
In the office of the Register of
Deeds within and for Tulsa County,
State of Oklahoma.
Recorded in Book 131, Page 106.
Consideration: $1.00 and other
valuable consideration.

GRANTING CLAUSE: Grant, bargain, sell and convey.

DESCRIPTION: The following described real estate situated in
the County of Tulsa, State of Oklahoma, to-wit:

Northwest Quarter of Section Sixteen (16), Town-
ship 19 North, Range Thirteen (13) East of the
Indian Base and Meridian, the same being the
allotment of Lucinda Hickory, deceased, and containing one hundred sixty acres, more or less,
as the case may be, according to the U. S. Plat
and Survey thereof.

WARRANTY: In fee simple, free and clear of all encumbrances,
and warrant the title to the same.

EXCEPTIONS: Any valid leases for oil and gas mining purposes
and coal mining purposes.

Witness to signature: Thomas Hickory
David Beaver
Henry W. Perryman
Joe Pigeon
C. O. Winterringer

ACKNOWLEDGED: On January 9, 1913, by Thomas Hickory, before
David Beaver, Notary Public, County of Tulsa,
State of Oklahoma.
(SEAL)   Commission expires Nov. 6, 1915.

Warranty deed transferring Lucinda Hickory's 160-acre allotment to Ethel Davis, January 9, 1913. The same day of her death.

Other grafters circled the Hickory household like vultures, deeds in hand, waiting for the perfect moment to pounce. But Sam had the edge — Jennie and Thomas trusted him. He wasn't just another outsider; he was already inside the circle. And he knew if he didn't act fast, someone else would take the swindle he'd been quietly setting up.

It never sat right with me how close he always seemed to be hovering just before the losses came. Lucinda's death... it came suddenly. And Sam? He was nearby, just like he was before.

What in the allotment hell was going on? Speculators moved swiftly while the local courts looked the other way, palms open, waiting for the highest bidder.

It was the Indian agent George McDaniel who entered the picture, doing his due diligence to challenge what was happening. One week after Lucinda's death, McDaniel filed a protest and dragged the Hickory family into a competency hearing to assess whether they were capable of managing their own affairs.

He was allegedly trying to protect the Hickory family from the very man they trusted. He challenged Sam Davis's actions and attempted to intervene.

Let me give some context to "Indian agent." It does not mean he was an Indian. It meant he was an Indian territory agent for the U.S. Secretary of the Interior. He was a non-Native.

At first, I was irritated when I discovered this. Who was George McDaniel to interfere in the Hickorys' lives, questioning their competency while they were mourning the loss of their child? The Hickorys didn't know him. And like other Creeks, I to believed that Sam Davis was their friend, looking out for their best interests. But as I looked deeper, I began to understand George's real concern: "Sam Davis."

McDaniel suspected Sam's reputation as a swindler, using his position to strip Indians of their wealth, all while flaunting his diamond rings and lavish lifestyle in Tulsa society. McDaniel seemed to be trying to save the Hickory's from Sam's conquest, even though his methods were intrusive and ill-timed.

The courts, however, were part of the problem. According to the Indian Rights Association's 1924 report titled "Oklahoma's Poor Rich Indians," the courts were just as responsible for the ongoing exploitation. Instead of protecting American Indians, they were making sure that everyone else got a piece of the Indian pie, everyone except the rightful heirs.

In February 1913, the Hickory family's competency was assessed before Judge Linn, who ultimately ruled that they were "no more or less competent than any other Indian." With that, the request for guardianship by George McDaniel was denied.

On the surface, this might have seemed like a victory—after all, who wants to be declared incompetent? Jennie & Thomas certainly didn't. So, in March of 1913, the Hickorys were found competent, and Sam Davis proceeded to claim the rents and royalties accrued and accruing from the lands of said deceased, "Lucinda," dating from February 18, 1913, for his wife Ethel.

Please, let's make no mistake here, this was not an act of love on Sam's part. Ethel was his shelter for the land grabs he was accumulating. After all, how would it have looked if he put it straight into his own name?

Also, there was no guarantee the Hickorys would've fared any better if George McDaniel had won guardianship.

The Allotment Era was a coconut shell game rigged from the start. It didn't matter who shuffled the pieces. Whether it was a so-called friend, a court-appointed agent, or a federal official, the outcome was almost always the same: Indians were dispossessed of their land by the *deeds of dishonest men*. The courts, blinded by greed, made the theft appear legal.

Guardianship wasn't about protection—it was about control. And in a game where the rules changed depending on who was watching, the Hickorys never stood a chance.

During the Allotment Era, many American Indians did not speak English at a high literacy rate. As a result, they were often deemed incompetent by the courts and appointed a guardian to manage their affairs. So, why weren't the Hickorys declared incompetent?

Here is my breakdown: if Judge Linn had found the Hickorys incompetent, then the sale of Lucinda's land would have been null and void. The Hickorys would have received the rents and royalties from their daughter's land, not Sam and his wife, Ethel.

George went to the Hickorys' home to warn them about his growing concerns over Sam Davis and what he was doing. But Sam was one step ahead—he had moved the Hickorys upriver, making them difficult to locate.

While Sam had them isolated, George suspected that he had coached them on what to say during the competency hearing, carefully preparing their answers to avoid raising any red flags about the swindle he had already set in motion.

The Hickorys were "obstinate" when answering the court's questions. It was becoming clear they did not know whom to trust.

The court was asking the grieving couple deeply problematic questions translated from a language they did not know into their Creek understanding.

They repeatedly grilled Jennie about how many 40-acre tracts made up 160 acres. Jennie and Thomas didn't speak or read English and certainly couldn't express mathematical calculations in that language. Thomas was just beginning to make efforts to learn English and the mathematical calculations that would be required. With that, Jennie left those matters to Thomas. But the court continued to badger her about the same mathematical calculations. Frustrated, Jennie said, "I want Tom to tell you what it is." It seemed the courts did not understand much of what Jennie had to say. They were confused. She was confused. It was all so confusing.

The interpreter, David Hodge, tried to explain to the court how Creeks use their language: "Backwards," Hodge explained. "It is about the same thing; if I say to you, 'you come to breakfast,' I would say, 'the breakfast comes to you.' It is the same thing, only just backwards; that is the way we use our language."

Exhausted by the repetitive questioning, Jennie lost her temper when attorney Mr. Norvell, asked her several times, "How much did you get for your interest?" She snapped, "I got $5,000; have you lost your ears? I told you that the time before."

When Mr. Norvell pressed further, asking, "How much is that an acre?" she quipped back, "You ought to know." And after that, she refused to answer any more questions.

Thomas wasn't treated any better. He was subjected to constant questions about his drinking habits. Even after testifying multiple times that he sometimes drank but never came home drunk, the questioning persisted in doing their best to show him as an incompetent drunk.

What was also disturbing were the questions—subtle, but unmistakable—suggesting Sam Davis's presence around the time of several mysterious deaths. No one said it outright, but I picked up on it.

They suspected Sam. Just like I do.

Of course, some believe it was his wife, Ethel, who pulled the strings. Maybe they worked hand in hand. Maybe they were Tulsa's first serial killers.

I wonder if Jennie ever knew what Sam had done. If she sensed that death...murder, followed in the wake of his deals. And I wonder if she knew...she would be next.

"Remembering Jennie"

Her name, her role in our family legacy, was almost forgotten. When I started this work, I was not sure who she was or how she would fit into the bigger picture of the story I was to tell. She was remembered but faintly so. Yet her role could well be the center or even the heart of what transpired for the Hickory family.

Her lash back at Tulsa County Court for ridiculing her in a competency hearing just a week after her eldest daughter's death. Even the trust she placed in Sam Davis, which kept at bay those who tried to warn her. Those were all lessons passed down through generations, though we didn't know where they originated.

Her dying wish to her children. Never sell the land. Her fervor and fortitude would go on for generations after her death. The fight was not over, it continues in her story, a reminder that justice cannot be ignored.

Jennie Hickory nee' Kuhne (Coney pronounced Cooney) the granddaughter of Tuckabache, my great grandmother. You are remembered, your fight continues.

Allotment...

*The Elders were right, but the Allotment Era still ensued,
and every Indian within the Mvskoke Nation Reservation
received 160 acres of land.*

*The newborns, the minors, the mixed bloods, the thin bloods,
the full bloods, the Freedman, and the five-dollar Indian too,
all received 160 acres of land.*

*Land to build their future in a
world that was not their own.
Land to have a family, land to call their home.*

*40 acres for a homestead and 120 acres for surplus,
all wrapped up in a government trust...?*

Chapter 8

THE DEMISE OF SAM DAVIS

And whose Oliver?

Samuel C. Davis

Sam Davis had it all— wealth, influence, and power. Part Creek and part white, he was a key player in Tulsa's oil boom, brokering land and oil deals with grafters. The web of Sam's life was tangled—affairs, wealth, and betrayal. Sam Davis was born in Indian Territory to a white father and a Creek mother, making him what was then called a *"half-breed."* He was heavily influenced by his father and the colonized world but was also deeply involved in his Creek culture.

As an educated *mix blood* Indian, Sam found it relatively easy to earn the trust of his Creek community. Even the Hickorys may well have named their son after him, Samuel C. Hickory.

However, he didn't seem to respect the Creek people. His involvement in Creek affairs and his role as the private secretary to former Creek Chief Legus Perryman gave him influence within the community. Yet, his choices suggest a self-serving ambition that puts his interests above loyalty to the Creeks.

Ambition filled the air in Indian Territory as it brought characters from all over the country. Many of whom were not successful elsewhere.

They found their opportunity here and took advantage of a culture of people who had different values of community.

Sam was very much the middleman in these deals. He could communicate with both worlds effectively. It was the way the settlers viewed the world that Sam seemed most enthralled with.

He was hungry for success and a life of privilege. The kind of success and privilege you find in the colonized world. Not the kind of success and privilege you would find in the Indian world. He wanted to be part of the Tulsa High Society. But for him to be part of their world, he would need Indian land—lots of *Dead Indian Land*.

The Hickorys were not his only victims; he took advantage of many Creeks who thought he was their friend. He was wheeling and dealing everyone.

Under the pretext of managing the Hickory family's affairs, he took over their finances, directed land deals for his own benefit, and became known for defrauding not only Indians —but possibly his white colleagues as well.

Something else struck me. With so much time "helping" other Creek Indians, it's no wonder Sam Davis didn't have time for Oliver. Or did Oliver not fit into his plans?

Whose Oliver? Sam's son by full-blood Creek, Louisa Partridge.

Sam's relationship with Louisa speaks volumes to me about his real views on Indians. They had a son together, Oliver Davis. Louisa died young, leaving Sam with his only son. But what was Sam planning? And was he too ashamed to raise his Indian son in a town that was chasing oil? Oliver, being Indian, did not fit into the life Sam was building. As depicted in the novel *Between Two Fires* by J.D. Colbert, perhaps these weren't his real views—perhaps it was part of his journey, caught between "two fires."

Sam took Oliver not to raise him but to leave him at an orphanage in Tulsa. It was an orphanage for Creek children managed by full-blood Rachel Perryman.

Rachel was well-known for taking in Creek orphans. She is known by locals and in history as Aunt

Rachel, a well-respected Creek who did not speak English.

But Oliver was not an orphan—he had a father, Sam Davis, who seemed to have other plans for himself that did not include raising his brown skinned son. Sam's decision to leave Oliver with Rachel implies a certain abandonment of his son and, perhaps, of his Creek heritage.

It's possible his new love interest, Ethel O'Reilly, did not look favorably on Sam having a child, let alone a son by another woman...and an Indian woman at that. So, Oliver was left at the orphanage. *Another story of the Allotment Era.*

Meanwhile, Sam moved on, marrying Ethel, with whom he had a daughter, Marjorie Irene Ethel Davis. In time, Ethel became a useful tool for Sam, while Marjorie went on to marry the mayor's son. Or perhaps his demise.

Like so many with power and money, it was never enough for Sam. He was a respected man of Tulsa, teaching Sunday school, and was becoming a Tulsa elite.

Ugg, but Sam turned his attention to the bottle, drinking heavily. His eye started to wander when he met a young woman, Daisy Carter, from Joplin, Missouri, with whom he began an illicit affair.

People were talking, and this caused a great scandal in Tulsa.

Humiliated and reeling from betrayal, Ethel Davis filed for divorce. Let me tell you— "humiliated and reeling from betrayal" doesn't sit well with a woman like Ethel—it's like mixing bleach and ammonia—kaboom! Honestly, I think this combination doesn't sit well with most women. Nevertheless, this scorned woman had them arrested for adultery.

But it was a weekend trip to Joplin, Missouri, to visit his mistress, Daisy Carter, that was the biggest part of the scandal. The two returned to Daisy's home from the theater to find a broken window.

Cautiously, they entered the house and heard someone upstairs. Sam rushed upstairs and Daisy followed lagging behind, while Daisy's mother waited below.

BOOM! BOOM!

Two loud shots from upstairs and Sam's wild, careless days had come to a sudden and violent end as he was shot to death during an altercation on December 18, 1916.

While his murder was never solved, speculations as to "who dun it" were everywhere. It could have been mayors, sons of mayors, judges, guardians, wards, a soon-to-be ex-wife, or even a mistress.

Sam got around, and he didn't seem to mind stirring the pot. He became an important man in Tulsa, so it was odd that his murder was never solved. Maybe because Sam was half Indian therefore merely a fatal causality that need not have answers. Or maybe, it was because he was a prominent person of Tulsa therefore swept under the carpet. Or was it because of who murdered him? But that story is for someone else to tell.

Now that Sam was murdered, who would look after the Hickory children's affairs? Who else could be so cold as to take advantage of young Indian children? The unfortunate answer to that was many. Many during those times would have vied for that position.

Keeping it in the family, within the same conspiracy, in early January 1917, Sam Davis's brother-in-law, Dr. JCW Bland, filed for guardianship of the Hickory children. By April 31, 1917, after seven years in probate, Bland sold the Tuckabache estate for $52,400, the equivalent of $1.2 million today.

Each of the Hickory children received approximately $14,444.00. This is equivalent to $353,088.00 today. Bland wasted no time giving it out to real estate developers and other locals in the community. It was taken out of each child's account. Young Sammie Hickory was left with $880 while his older sister, Sallie, was left with a mere $88. I have not found the financial records for my grandmother, Louina Hickory, but it is said she squandered the money.

Unlikely! The guardian most likely used the money for the same type of business affairs that her brother and sister's money was used for. Or perhaps he kept it himself. Louina was still just a kid, a minor, who did not have access to her money.

This isn't hearsay. It's their own writing and their own testimony.

And this is where another huge problem lies. Guardians would live off and benefit from minor Indians using up all their money, selling their estates, leaving them with nothing. By the time the minor became of age they had nothing left and for some nothing but debt.

COPY

County of Tulsa
STATE OF OKLAHOMA } ss TO THE JUDGES OF THE COUNTY COURT OF
SAID COUNTY.

GUARDIAN'S ANNUAL REPORT.

The undersigned, J. C. W. Bland, guardian of Sallie Hickory would respectfully submit to the court the following report of his acts and doings as such guardian from February 7th, 1917 to July 10th, 1917. GUARDIAN charges himself with the following, to-wit:

SEMI- ANNUAL REPORT.

DATE Month, Day, Year		ITEMS OF RECEIPT	AMOUNT	TOTAL AMT.
April 30	1917	Lionel E. E. Aaronson		
		Check - land sale	1280.89	
May 1	"	" "	13333.33	
July 6	"	A. H. Mathews et al.		
		refund out of check on		
		payment	100.00	
		Total amount of moneys received or collected		$14,714.22

COSTRA

Guardian asks to be credited with the following sums, paid out as per receipts exhibited.

DATE Month, Day, Year			ITEMS PAID OUT	AMOUNT	TOTAL AMT.
May 1	1917	1	To Clerk County Court Court Costs	20.00	
" 1	"	2	To Sister Superior School expenses	71.34	
" 5	"	3	To O. D. Miller Real Estate Loan	2000.00	
" 17	"	4	To Davidson, Williams, Grimes and Bell Fees court order	400.00	
" 19	"	5	To James H. Sykes Fees court order	1500.00	
" 26	"	6	To Lewis B. Wood Realty Company Real Estate Loan	3000.00	
June 21	"	7	To Thomas Hickory Expenses	15.00	
July 3	"	8	To Lewis B. Wood Realty Co. R. E. Loan	5000.00	
" 6	"	9	To A. H. Mathews, et al. R. E. Loan	1500.00	
" 7	"	10	To Sallie Hickory For clothes	20.00	
" 7	"	11	Thomas Hickory for maintenance 5 yrs.	1000.00	
			Total amount paid out		$14626.34
			Total amount received	$14714.22	$14714.22
			" " paid out	$14626.34	$14626.34
			Balance due ward	$87.98	$87.98

Guardian's Annual Report, J.C.W. Bland for Sallie Hickory, balance due ward $87.98.
February 7–July 10, 1917 (Tulsa County Court).

I never agreed to the exchanging of lands, and I never agreed to the allotting of lands. I knew it would never do for my people... I can't speak the tongue. I can't read, I can't write... I am notifying you of these things because your Government officials told me they would take care of my relations with the Government — and they ought to be taking care of them as they promised."

— *Chitto Harjo*, *testimony before the U.S. Senate Committee on Indian Affairs, Washington, D.C., 1906*

Chapter 9

LOUINA & THE PROMISE

Her mom's dying wish.

Louina Sunday, nee Hickory, my grandmother had an extraordinary life. Not extraordinary in the sense of her accomplishments, but in the sense of her survival. When our tribal lands were divided up into individual land allotments in April of 1899 due to an amendment to the Dawes Act called the Curtis Act, she received her own 160 acres of land in 1905 as a newborn.

It's a common misconception that the Dawes Act forced the division of our communal lands. In truth, the Five Civilized Tribes were excluded from that legislation. It was the 1898 Curtis Act—and its devastating amendments—that dismantled our systems of self-governance and wreaked havoc on our Native legacies.

If you were part of the Dawes Roll of Muscogee (Creek) Nation, known at the time as Creek Nation, then you received 160 acres of land, 40 acres for a homestead and 120 acres of surplus. Which seems like a great idea on paper, 160 acres tax-exempt for 25 years. It should have been an opportunity for stability, even prosperity.

For my ancestors, it was a fight for survival during assimilation so they could exist in a changing world. Existing was the only expectation, but even that became inconsequential as this was merely a facade, setting the stage for our decline.

Louina was born just in the midst of land allotment, and her 160-acre allotment is in present-day Sand Springs, Oklahoma, which is controlled by the owners of the Flying G Ranch. The family still has ownership of approx. 11 acres that they do not have access to. We probably won't get into that story in this book, but believe me when I tell you, there is a story there, too.

Like her ancestors before her, Louina was caught in the grip of the government's broken promises. Her childhood was cut short as government policies were being manipulated by settlers. Louina became a voice for her family, communicating their decisions to the white settlers.

She experienced tremendous loss in her young life with the death of her older sister, Lucinda. She and her younger sister, Sallie, were sent to St. Elizabeths in Purcell, Oklahoma, to an Indian Boarding school shortly after Lucinda's death. So, during a time of deep grief, when the Hickory family needed each other the most, they were ripped apart. Jennie and Thomas Hickory were left alone, their children scattered. Their youngest son, Sammie C. Hickory, was sent to live with Sallie Morrison, a half-Creek, half-white woman, and then another woman after her. The loss of family, in every sense, must have been unbearable.

Before Jennie's death, she was fast becoming a very wealthy heiress with her interests in the Tuckabache estate, which included Ned Tuckabatchie's 160 acres, Tom Coney's estate, her father's estate, her daughter, Lucinda's estate, and her own 160 acre allotment which was the family's residence.

For the family, there was also Thomas's 160 acres and Louina's 160 acres. It was a great wealth that seemingly turned her and her family into targets.

As Jennie lay dying, she told her daughter never to sell their land. This was important to Louina, and she fought long and she fought hard...Louina did everything she could to keep her mother's dying wish.

I think of all my great-grandmother Jennie endured, and how much that dying request must have meant to her. She saw what was unfolding—she wanted to protect her children. The land was already slipping away, following a string of early deaths shrouded in secrecy.

What chills me most...is how little the dying wish of a young Indian mother mattered to the grifters and grafters. How easily they dismissed her final plea.

The disregard for Jennie Hickory's plea eventually spiraled the family into poverty. It led to endless legal battles that never stopped.

Their story is one of relentless struggle. The grafters' pursuit of the Hickory estate was nothing short of horrific—a violation so pervasive it continues to weigh heavily, even now.

In Muscogee (Creek) culture, women are the property owners, and children inherit their mother's status. Lina (Tuckabache's wife), my third great grandmother, belonged to the Tribal Town Quassertey (2), so would her daughter Sallie Coney, my great-grandmother, Jennie Hickory, also belonged to the Tribal Town Quassartey (2), as did her daughter, Louina Sunday (my grandmother), my mother; Sallie Keblish, and now, me, Tatianna K. Duncan. Sadly, I must confess that my Tribal Town, Quassartey, is where I am from—it is not where I have been. At least, not yet.

Naturally, it made sense for the family to settle on Jennie's allotment. This is where their home was built, a home that Thomas Hickory constructed with his own hands. It was where Lucinda met an untimely death—where Jennie passed too soon—and from where the children were sent away to Indian Boarding school. It was also where Thomas was left to grieve... alone. As Jennie died two years almost to the date of her daughter's death. January 3, 1915.

More than a house; it should have been their refuge in good times and bad, a place they could always return to, their security in every sense of the word.

Like Tuckabache's land, which was sought after for its pristine beauty, Jennie's property was a prime target for land grabbers eager to build a housing development. Located at 31st and Lewis, it became a battleground over inheritance, honor, and survival.

As previously discussed, Jennie entrusted her daughter, Louina, with a solemn promise: to never sell the land, to hold onto it. It was their legacy. Louina took this charge to heart, fighting fiercely to protect what her mother had left behind. This is her statement to the Tulsa County Court in a battle for their home.

My name is Louina Hickory. I am a sister of Sallie and Sammie Hickory. We are the heirs of Jennie Hickory, deceased. We are the minors, whose lands are attempting to be sold by the guardian at this time. Sallie and I are attending the convent school at Purcell, Oklahoma. Sammie is staying with Mrs. Sallie Morrison, near Broken Arrow. I am 15 years of age. I have been attending school at Purcell for the last four years. Sallie, Sammie, and I inherited this land from my mother, Jennie Hickory. I would like to hold the land. I don't want the land sold. I am the oldest one of the minors who owns this land. I talked with my mother in regard to this land before she died. [vi]

It seemed like a triumph. The Tulsa County Court agreed with Louina, denying the sale of their home. For a moment, it felt like justice had finally been served. But it wasn't the end—not even close.

My grandmother, just 15 years old, stood in that courtroom and testified with confidence about her family's intentions, just as her dying mother had expressed them. What courage it must have taken to carry that responsibility! I feel an immense sense of pride knowing the strength from which I come. Her words were an act of heroism, a clear demand for what was rightfully theirs. So why was this not enough?

The guardian, Dr. JCW Bland, and his associate, real estate developer J.O. Campbell, appealed the county court's decision to the district court.

The district court overturned the ruling, a cruel reversal that threatened to sever the Hickory family from their home once more.

Desperate to defend their rights, the Hickory family, with attorney John Wakely, took the fight to the Oklahoma Supreme Court and won a precedent-setting victory.

Relieved and ready to return, Thomas looked forward to spending the summer with his children, who were home from boarding school. The past few years had been marked by relentless heartache and legal battles—the loss of his eldest daughter, Lucinda, and his wife, Jennie, weighing heavily on his heart. He missed the comfort of the home he had built for his family, the place that should have been their sanctuary.

This land was supposed to be secure. Surely this, of all things, could not be taken from them. After all, wasn't this the basis of the promises made by the colonized world?

Providing food, shelter, and safety for one's family—a place to call their own. Being full-blood, their homestead and surplus lands should have been protected for at least 25 years. These protections were called "restrictions." But this so-called "protective measure" lasted not even 20 years. Within 20 years of allotment, 80-90% of Indian land was in the hands of non-Natives.

The Hickory family was part of these despairing stats. The Hickory's never asked for more than what was just.

But instead of the comfort of home, Thomas was met with hostility. Strangers stood on his land, their faces wrought with anger, shouting for him to leave. They chased him and his children away from their home—as if they were the intruders.

I'm horrified!

While Bland couldn't sell the Hickory home, he did make a shady deal with Thomas.

Not only did Bland have Thomas sell his interest in his wife's land to their children, effectively cutting him out of all decision-making. He then in turn, used the kids being away at Indian Boarding school, as a reason to lease out their home.

These are the types of land deals that raise questions. It was clear Thomas didn't understand the land transaction, as he constantly tried to go back home.

Even with Thomas out of the picture, the battle for the Hickory estate was far from over. A struggle over land, legacy, and justice continued to unfold, with new challenges waiting at every turn.

Making a magnanimous statement about the mother's deathbed wish, her Indian heritage, and the district court's responsibility to listen to the young Indian girl turned out to be little more than a sham.

The Oklahoma Supreme Court remanded the case to the Tulsa District Court, instructing them to "consider" these points without offering a clear resolution.

With the decision back in the lower court, the Hickory family once again found themselves stripped of their home—a devastating blow to a family already worn down by years of struggle. Yet, the fight was not over.

That is why...

That is why...there is a cloud on the title,
there is a cloud on the deed,

oh dear, oh my goodness, what could this mean?!

There must be a "Dead Indian" tied to your land.
A history unspoken that we must understand.

Chapter 10

In Walks Poo Sunday

Taking a stand for his family

Let's take a quick break from my Hickory family and talk about the Sundays. When I visited the National Archives in Kansas, I was surprised to learn that the boarding schools tracked more than just behavior and grades— they tracked allotments. Children weren't always allowed to return home for the summer.

"Johnnie has misbehaved; he cannot return home."

"Tom's parents are dead; he has no home to return to."

"Shelley's parents are undesirable. She doesn't need to go home."

These decisions lacked humanity. Home became a conditional place, and the needs of the family were not relevant. The deeper I read, the more it became clear: the boarding school system was not separate from the allotment system. They were an extension of each other.

One took the home, the other took the children, and the family...paid the price.

My great-grandfather, (William) Poo Sunday, drew a line in the sand. He was a U.S. Marshal, fluent in Cherokee, Creek, and English. When Haskell boarding school tried to keep his sons from coming home for the summer—because trust me, the Sunday boys could be a handful—he didn't write a polite letter. He showed up in person.

He demanded that his children be released, telling the school that his wife was sick from missing her boys—and that he would not return home without them.

The school labeled him "unsavory." It must have been something he said, as they noted his foul language and criticized his conduct in official records.

But what they were really saying was: he disrespected their authority. He was an Indian father who challenged their right to decide when, or if, he could see his children. And they didn't like that.

The Sunday boys were intelligent, strong-willed, and restless in captivity. They didn't take well to being held by boarding schools. One would become a local rodeo celebrity in Tulsa, The Tulsa Trail Riders. One would serve in the military. And one was studious and serious about his future. A few would run wild and become bank robbers in a society that had already labeled them threats. But it still wasn't okay that they robbed banks they spent time in the Oklahoma State Penitentiary in McAlister, Oklahoma. No matter their paths, the common thread was this: they weren't broken... they were surviving.

That day, when Poo Sunday stood at the schoolhouse and demanded his children, it wasn't just about a summer visit — it was an act of defiance. Even a U.S. Marshal, in their eyes, was still an Indian to be put in his place.

Where were Indian families supposed to turn for solace, for support, when even their grief was used against them? Land, language, and now children were all regulated by forms, guardians, and institutional rules. The cruelty wasn't just in the policies—it was in the precision.

A precision that cut to the core of Indian families already being torn apart by a world that dismissed everything about them, from their traditions to the color of their skin.

Moving forward...

*The progressive leadership said yes, we must progress,
lest we be forgotten.*

The traditional leadership saw their world rapidly changing.

*Unable to stop the change,
they were determined to keep their language and traditions.*

*They knew to take stock
as they were about to face... culture shock.*

Chapter 11

The Family Home

It wasn't just swindle, it was outright theft

What happens next to me is inconceivable. Not long after Lucinda's death, the rest of the Hickory children were sent away to Indian boarding school. I ask myself: Was this for their protection or their "education," or was it to weaken the family to keep them from being strong enough to stop what was happening to them?

Jennie and Thomas were left alone, in a house was once meant for a happy family, a home where their children should have been running across their 160-acre farm, living, learning, and thriving instead of merely surviving in Indian Boarding school while grown men battle your little girls for their home.

I can't begin to imagine the depth of their grief, though I try. This must have been the lowest point in their lives. I can almost feel their pain, but pull back because why would anyone willingly allow themselves to feel such sorrow? Yet they had no choice.

I don't have insight into their day-to-day routine, but I can only imagine the racism they faced in what was supposed to be Indian Territory, a place meant to be a new beginning, not a new battleground.

If alcoholism has affected Native communities, it's important to recognize the grief and generational trauma that was forced upon us. This doesn't excuse substance abuse, but it explains the roots of it — and naming those roots is part of healing. With the education we have today, we owe it to ourselves not to use trauma as a reason to harm our own lives.

I've faced those struggles. I've lost old friends and made new ones in the same night — and no, that's never the sign of a good evening. Yes, alcohol was involved. I'm not saying drinking is some kind of Indian rite of passage. It isn't. It has added nothing to my life; if anything, it has taken time I can't get back. Anything done responsibly can be enjoyable — I just don't want anyone walking away thinking being Indian is an excuse to drink.

And yet, in a mixed crowd, there's always some dipwad who will make a "firewater" joke while holding their own drink. Why is my glass different from theirs? I suppose they think it's cute.

I often think of what Thomas went through. How was he supposed to handle any of it?

His wife dead. His eldest daughter dead. His remaining children sent away. His language unrecognized. His rights unprotected. His land under siege. This was the beginning of the most critical battle of his life — the fight for the Hickory home.

With the death of Jennie, whose allotment was foundational to not just her family but to the generations that were to come. It was the foundation on which family legacy is built—It was home—the core to every society.

In the movie Gone with the Wind, Scarlett O'Hara could face anything and all odds as long as she could return to her family home. It was actually a plantation but let me continue. After all she had been through with death, war, and the wrong love. Scarlett finally realized her true love. Too bad Rhett was done with her by the time she made that revelation. So, when he tells her, "Frankly, my dear, I don't give a damn!" Scarlett is now crushed. ALL is lost, but then she remembers "Tarra," the family plantation. For *her,* it was home, it was her foundation, their family's legacy. And when all else failed, all she wanted was to go back home–home to Tarra. After all, "home is where the heart is."

Louina and Sallie must have had similar feelings about their home after being away at Boarding School. They just wanted to get back home. Home with family and traditions. Sharing great stories, making and eating incredible meals. Also, the laughter—we cannot forget the laughter that only family seems to understand. At least, in Native families. Yet by 1919, they never return home again. Frankly, my dears, it's because of the Scarlett O'Haras or in Oklahoma's case, the swindlers.

By 1915, in less than 15 years of land being allotted, six landowning ancestors are dead. All under unknown or mysterious circumstances.

As for land, 960 acres of land have been either taken or are in probate to be taken.

The legal battle over Jennie Hickory's property was relentless. How many times should one family have to say, "I don't want to sell my land," before the land grabbers listened? In Indian Territory, at least one more time...always. But they never did— listen—or more likely, they simply didn't care.

Thomas Hickory was yet another exceptional story of survival. All my ancestors carry strength in their stories, but to me, Thomas takes the cake. He is true resilience. If he'd been fluent in English, perhaps his story, our story, would have turned out differently — but he was up against an impossible tide.

His world was torn apart piece by piece–the systems meant to protect him became the very channels used to undermine him. And the grafters didn't just exploit loopholes — they created them.

The system failed him on every level, and from this side of history, it feels intentional.

And for Indian families, the land wasn't the only loss–deaths shrouded in secrecy became a convenient tool for those eager to take everything from them. Indian life seemed inconsequential merely an obstacle to "progress."

And the graft was on…

Over and over, again and again, the claim would be the same.

No, I do not want to sell my land, the Indian would proclaim!

I want to hold on to my land the Indian did demand.

I want to keep my home, that sits on my family's land!

Chapter 12

DOSES OF BETRAYAL

The business of killing Indians for land

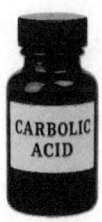

Poisoning Indians was common knowledge in my world, a painful part of our oral history. But seeing it printed in black and white, from a time when so many of our ancestors had fatal outcomes under questionable circumstances, it brought that history to the surface and set it in stone. It was no longer just a story passed down through generations; it was proof that our oral history was not a mere tale from long ago but the record of real crimes—unsolved—unrecognized—and dismissed by society without justice.

May 1, 1913, the *Tulsa World* reports on a poison plot that happened in Choctaw Nation which is in southeast Oklahoma. The article reports that *scores of Indians have been put out of the way by the poison route since statehood.*

> **Poisoning Indians a Business?**
>
> It is the claim of the officers that scores of Indians have been put out of the way by the poison route since statehood. In every instance it was found that the dead Indian had made a land grafter or some undesirable his beneficiary, and that his death occurred shortly after the will was executed.
>
> County Attorney Warren stated today that he had a sure case against the men arrested today and that other arrests would be made.
>
> For more than a year officials have been working on what they believed was a systematic plot to get aged Indians to make an agreement with grafters, or worse, whereby the grafter was to pay to the Indian a stated amount of cash each month as long as the Indian lived and the Indian at the same time was induced to make a will with the party furnishing the money as the beneficiary. The current monthly stipend is said to have been $10, but in each instance the Indian making such an agreement lived only a few months, and it was this that first led to an investigation.

"Poison Plot Is Now Unearthed." This front-page story in the Tulsa World (May 1, 1913) exposed allegations of systematic poisonings of Indians in Oklahoma after statehood. Officials reported a pattern, aged Indians induced to make wills naming white beneficiaries, followed by sudden suspicious deaths. The article reflects the growing awareness — though not always action — of how corruption and violence were tied to land and inheritance during the Allotment Era.

In my heart and soul, I believe Tuckabache, Tom Coney, and Lucinda Hickory were murdered—their deaths surrounded by red flags and unanswered questions.

While I can't be certain about my great-grandmother, Jennie Hickory, I wouldn't be surprised if she, too, was a victim when we see how ferociously grafters came after her land when she died.

There were many other forms of poising besides carbolic acid, it just so happened, carbolic acid pertains to this story. From a quick internet search:

<u>Symptoms of poisoning:</u>

Nausea and vomiting Severe abdominal pain

Diarrhea, Dizziness and confusion

Headache Convulsions

Unconsciousness Difficulty breathing

Weak or irregular heartbeat *Death*

The Spirit of the
Indian Family Attacked

Families were left impoverished; families were left destitute.
Men were unusually imprisoned, while wives became widows,
children became orphans, and all were displaced from a place
that was their home.

Indian Boarding schools and stolen allotted lands.
Indians were dying at a higher rate than most any other man.

Once wealthy in spirit, and then wealthy in land;
all heartlessly stolen by despicable man.

Chapter 13

"FRIENDS OF THE INDIAN"
OR
"DEAD INDIAN"

Kill the Indian, save the man
Kill the Indian, take the land

Many who called themselves "Friends of the Indian"—politicians, lawyers, missionaries—claimed to be on our side. But that friendship meant assimilation, taking our land, and remaking us in an inferior image of themselves.

In their minds, they were helping, even saving us, but this kind of friendship meant loss of culture.

For every "Friend of the Indian," there were a "Dozen Dead Indians." One was supposed to protect us.

"FRIENDS OF THE INDIAN"
OR
"DEAD INDIAN"

The other to abolish us. In the end, they worked hand in hand.

Whether they came as friends or a grafter, the result was the same—destroy everything about us and take whatever we had.

With the deaths of Tuckabache, Ned Tuckabatchie, Moses Coney, Tom Coney, Lucinda Hickory, and Jennie Hickory, the land grabbers were anxious to get hold of their land. This land became known as "Dead Indian land"—a term frequently used to describe land owned by a deceased Indian. Municipalities were eager to acquire this land for taxpayers.

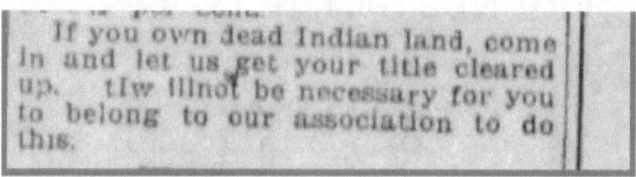

Tulsa World (Tulsa, OK), July 12, 1918, p. 3.
An ad inviting the public to profit from "dead Indian land" — a phrase so common in early Oklahoma that it disguised theft as business.

Even today, certain real estate professionals use the term "Dead Indian" when referring to land with a clouded title.

Investigating these unethical practices and the people who preyed on my ancestors has been tough. When I use the word "ancestors," it feels like I'm speaking of some distant, mystical past. But the

Hickorys who became the Sundays were my family— are my family.

My grandmother, though she died before I was born, is still a close connection to me. My Aunt Sallie lived only miles away, she and her husband, Uncle Jess, would come over for holiday meals and Sunday visits. We all went to Church together.

Their grandson, my cousin Jess E. Sunday, was a good friend and classmate. His little sister, again my cousin, is also a good friend of mine.

Ancestors often seem like they belong to a time long ago, but for me, this wasn't so long ago. It brings me to the present. So much so that when the park, Gathering Place, tried to honor the original allottees whose land they now sit on, one being Tuckabache, they had the insensitivity to ask my mother and me, "Do we think Tuckabache would be happy with what his land has become today—a place for everyone?"

This question inspired the poem in a manifesto I wrote about the Allotment Era, which you can find between paragraphs throughout this book. There is still a deep lack of education about the Allotment Era. If you're a Native descendant connected to this history, you might be all too familiar with it.

I often wonder where the descendants of the guardians are—the ones who oversaw the land and legal affairs of Native families. I wish they would come forward, and we could have an open discussion.

I'm not sure why this matters to me, but it does.

"FRIENDS OF THE INDIAN"
OR
"DEAD INDIAN"

I once spoke on the phone with the grandson, or perhaps the great-grandson, of Dr. JCW Bland. He claimed he didn't know much about Dr. Bland or his grandmother, Sue Bland. He is part Creek as was his grandmother, Sue. We were supposed to stay in touch, but he never answered me again.

Maybe some believe certain things are better left in the past. But for me, I seek justice for my family. Justice that, as Indians, we know doesn't exist—not in the way it should.

Let's have a short conversation on religion and those friends.

I was raised in a Catholic household — my dad Russian Orthodox, my mom Catholic — and I never questioned my religion growing up. It is a beautiful faith and was a strong foundation of my upbringing. I am not here to diminish it or any other religion. But I am in discernment as I often wonder: what was my great-grandmother, Jennie Hickory's religion? What was Tuckabache's? That is the faith I want to understand.

As a young mother, I taught Catholicism to children in different grades, and I loved it. But even then, something felt missing. I remember being inspired when I first learned about Saint Katharine Drexel, a wealthy heiress who became a nun and devoted her fortune to Catholic schools for Indians and African Americans. In the height of my Catholic spirituality, I admired her. There was an enthusiasm that maybe my grandmother had met her. But I learned while her money funded much of St. Elizabeth's Boarding School in Purcell, her visits there were in 1902 and in 1905. Later, though, I wondered if she was also one of those so-called "Friends of the Indian" — people who believed our acceptance depended on surrendering our own culture to embrace theirs. We could belong, but only if we succumbed to their religion. This has sent me into discernment.

Her sainthood was celebrated due to her intrusion on our Indian culture. She believed she was doing good but in reality, she funded the destruction of not only sovereignty but the right to exist as Indians. St. Katharine Drexel was canonized by Pope John Paul II on October 1, 2000. The Catholic Church recognized her for a life of "heroic virtue," her founding of the Sisters of the Blessed Sacrament in 1891, and the miracles attributed to her intercession after death. She spent her fortune — more than $20 million in early 20th-century dollars — to build schools, churches, and missions for Native Americans and African Americans. In the eyes of the Church, her sainthood was a celebration of service to the marginalized.

But from where I stand, that service came at a cost. She believed she was doing good, yet the schools and missions she funded often required Indians to abandon their language, culture, and beliefs in exchange for acceptance. Her canonization may have been celebrated in Rome, but for us it represents another chapter in the destruction of our right to exist as Indians on our own terms.

As Indian Boarding schools are known for the abuse they inflicted on young Indian children, I have not heard that Louina or her sister had such experiences. But I want to be clear, I just don't know.

At the same time, I can't dismiss the fact that her Catholic faith gave my mother strength. Growing up without her own mother, Catholic education and her devotion to the Blessed Mother Mary and faith in Jesus Christ carried her through the darkest times of her life. Faith was and is her anchor.

During my mother's formative years as a child, she would have attended Mass in Latin — as did every Catholic around the world until the 1960s, when the Second Vatican Council permitted the use of the vernacular. That change came too late for her. In those years, not only Indians but even white Catholics in America worshiped in a tongue they could not fully understand. For my family, this meant one more barrier to our language.

I look at other Indians who found a different path in smaller Protestant churches. Many of them could and still do pray and sing in Creek, connecting Christianity with their Mvskoke culture. But for Catholics like us, that integration wasn't allowed. Latin was the only voice in our prayers.

The legacy of my ancestors...

*When Gathering Place,
which is where my family's inheritance lay, asked would
Tuckabache be happy with what his land has become today,*

"A place for everyone!"

*I felt my facial expression and wanted to sink deep into
depression as my thoughts went to Tuckabache,
my third great grandfather.*

*I was bewildered, I was perplexed.
What was this question?*

You won't like what I have to say next!

*His grandchildren and great granddaughter
met untimely deaths,
Leaving me to believe it was
murder in their ominous quest.*

Upon his death, old and frail,
his last days must have felt like hell.
As he too, may have been the victim of foul play.

There was theft and betrayal.
There was so much disruption.
His family lost all, due to the corruption.

The greed, the graft, murder, and the swindle.
Everything they possessed seemed to dwindle.

The culture he fought for is almost non-existent.
Generations still suffer from the grafter's persistence.
Tuckabache had hope his descendants would not have to cope,
With the vultures who were stealing our Mvskoke culture.

Forced to assimilate,
as descendants we can only relate,
to the Indian blood that runs through our veins.

Forced into submission we have lost our traditions
and do not know our Mvskoke ways.

So, the answer to the question,
"would Tuckabache be happy with what
his land has become today,"

"A place for everyone."

Frustrated, I shake my head in dismay.
For in my heart and soul I can only say, No!
I must convey he'd be outraged
by just how bad things have become.

In disbelief he'd have to face just how far
the corruption had run.

Chapter 14

THOMAS HICKORY

A Tale of the Allotment Era

In a modest-sized home that housed a large family, was a haven built on perseverance, held together by resilience, in the face of unimaginable loss.

Inside, there was a small room where the door always seemed to be open, welcoming anyone who wanted to stop in.

There, they would find an older man, his late sixties marked by a lifetime of hardships and triumphs. His dark brown skin, a head full of silver hair, and an amputated leg told of years spent enduring and surviving.

Thomas Hickory, or "Papa," as the family lovingly called him, sat in that room playing solitaire with a deck of old, worn-out cards. The numbers were barely visible; the edges frayed from years of constant use.

His daughter often offered to buy him a new deck, but he always refused. In a world that had taken so much from him, perhaps those cards were something familiar. Maybe they had been through a lot together. Maybe they were symbols of his quiet determination his unwillingness to let go of what was still his.

His grandchildren adored him, even if they couldn't hold long conversations. Papa only spoke Creek, and they were only allowed to speak English. But language was never a barrier to love or understanding. They respected him deeply—he was the cornerstone of the family.

But what was it like for Papa, not able to pass on his traditions or his language? Not able to share his stories? I cannot imagine the loneliness he must have felt — in a home full of his grandchildren who could not understand him. To me, that is a true travesty.

Now a truth from the past, full of stories and history—stories that today can only be uncovered through documents, newspaper clippings, and tales from elders' storytelling.

Papa was protective of his family — fiercely so. It was said he once cut a man from one side of his gut to the other for disrespecting his daughter.

To the outsiders dismantling his life, he was labeled improvident, a drunk, and a man unfit to manage his affairs. But those labels were lies, tools of a system designed to strip him of his dignity and his land.

Thomas Hickory lived through the heart of the Allotment Era, a treacherous time when wretched intruders demolished everything he tried to build.

He had seen the worst of humanity: judges, lawyers, preachers, city leaders, and entrepreneurs who called themselves righteous while stealing the foundation of his world.

These were the deeds of dishonest men. I call them the "founding fathers of Tulsa." They were not heroes. They were opportunists.

And yet, despite their cruelty, Papa remained. He refused to let their actions define him, holding onto his family, his humor, and his pride.

Reflecting on Papa Hickory, I am struck by his strength and fortitude. For the past 10 years, I've delved into the tangled web of his business affairs, uncovering the corruption that shadowed his life. The more documents I uncover, the louder I want to scream. The injustice that unfolded before him wasn't hidden—it was blatant, systematic, and callously ignored.

As their world was rapidly changing around them, the sources they needed to keep up were systematically stripped away. With strength and resolve, they picked themselves up and moved forward as best they could. And that's what we've done ever since.

I can only imagine the courage it took to keep going — to watch everything slip away while those in power looked the other way. At some point, strength wasn't enough. So, it was time to seek out an attorney. The formal complaint was filed by Thomas Hickory himself:

"The three children who survived their mother, together with this complainant, are wrongfully and unlawfully kept out of their said home... The house on said premises having been built by this complainant, who has no home now, and is living on charity."

Living on charity...this was a wealthy family! The emotional weight of reading this document was overwhelming. But even that couldn't compare to the weight of the lived experience. Processing this injustice left me in disbelief.

It was in reading these documents that I first began to put myself into the Allotment Era. I couldn't help but wonder: How, as Thomas's great-granddaughter, could I have protected him?

For the first time, I felt connected to Thomas as a real person—as a true elder, not a ghost of the past.

But the grifters and grafters spoke of my great-grandfather, and so many other Indian men, as "drunks," "improvident," or "unintelligent." These words failed to capture the complexity of their lives or their capabilities. Many Indians at that time not only spoke their language, but were multilingual, speaking in Creek, Cherokee, Osage, Choctaw, and some English too.

They were navigating in a society that was intentionally trying to break them. This society called Papa improvident while they quietly drained him of his money and land. They labeled him a drunk but refused to see that he's a grieving man. They inflicted immeasurable harm on him, his legacy, and his family.

His family said he was quiet. He would wait until all the kids were fed before he would eat. They never saw him drunk, but they knew when he went to town to be with the other Creek citizens...well...they knew it just was not their business.

He always came home sober, sometimes dropped off by the police, who were very kind to him. He was a good man.

To his family, he was their "papa," and they loved him.

As I piece together his story, I realize Papa Hickory's resilience and strength in surviving the Allotment Era amid unimaginable destruction— now that's a lesson worth learning!

Chapter 15

BOOMERS, SOONERS, AND BROKEN PROMISES

A state built on corruption

"Boomer...Sooner!!" Should I expect anything different from a state that celebrates an action such as "the Sooners?" This is not an attack on a football team or its fans, but rather a critique of an ideology that glorifies land theft and cheating as signs of resourcefulness. "Boomer" originally referred to those who agitated for the opening of Indian lands for white settlement, disregarding treaties and tribal ownership.

Even worse, "Sooner," was a term given to those who staked their claims on Indian lands, which had been opened up for white settlement, before they were legally allowed to do so, jumping the gun to steal the best parcels for themselves. Yet somehow, over time, this disregard for the law has turned into a celebration of victory.

It's hard not to be swept up in the excitement of hearing "Boomer Sooner" ringing from the stands—the cry sounding powerful, like a call to action, full of pride and community.

The colors crimson and cream are beautiful, and my favorite team colors. But, to some of us, the phrase "Boomer Sooner" is a reminder of the unsettling past of land runs and the rush to claim Indian land, which brought with it unsavory characters.

It's not an attack on the passionate Sooner fans, but rather a call to reflect on the deeper history behind that pride.

But these were the kinds of people Thomas Hickory and other Native Americans faced, opportunists who saw Indian land as a means to their legacy, never considering the lives that were tied to it. And while the names and faces may have changed, their descendants and their legacies continue to shape our present, repeating the past in ways that still haunt us today.

If you're waiting for a happy ending, know that we're still working on one. For now, this is a story of survival against all odds, and the battle is far from over.

With Dr. Bland controlling Thomas's finances and having dispossessed him of his home, Thomas found himself destitute, out on the streets, and penniless.

It was Louina, his daughter, fresh home from Indian boarding school, who stepped up to help her father. I can only imagine how upsetting this must have been for Louina and Sallie: to return home and see how the so-called "progress" of Tulsa had torn their family apart and reduced their wealth to nothing.

In 1917, as the struggle over the Hickory family land escalated, Bland made a move to strip Thomas Hickory of any rights to his family's allotment. This wasn't a mere oversight. It was a deliberate maneuver.

As mentioned earlier, Bland—posing as a protector—tightened his grip once again. By transferring Thomas's interest in his wife's land to his children—of whom he conveniently served as guardian—he ensured that no adult oversight would stand in his way. With no one to challenge his authority, he gained complete control over the family's property, free to manipulate it as he pleased.

These were intentional acts of swindle, all while the courts turned a blind eye, probably receiving a cut under the table. Stolen in broad daylight by men who Tulsa has celebrated in its history.

What struck Louina—and, frankly, me—was the brazen theft right under their noses. While her family faced homelessness, Louina discovered that her store account had been used without her knowledge while she was away at school in Santa Fe, New Mexico. As she began to uncover the full scope of their situation, what she found was disheartening. The very accounts meant to support her family had become the pocket cash of greedy men. Store accounts, bank accounts—nothing was untouched. And apparently, seeking justice was going to be expensive too. Their attorney, John Wakely, who had stepped in to bring order to the chaos, demanded fifty percent of whatever he could recover. The damage was deep.

Charges totaling $300—a staggering amount equivalent to more than $5,000 today—were used to buy kindred women's wear she never purchased.

And her father's account was no better: checks totaling $1,400 (around $24,600 in today's value) were missing.

Louina also informed Wakely that there was an allowance of some $5,000.00 for an attorney's fee against the Hickory minors. An equivalent of $119,000.00 today. Her fears were that a similar allowance by reason of the sale of her mother's land that is being carried out against her will was about to happen again.

While Wakely with his own 50% of whatever he "recovered agenda" was there to assist, the Department of the Interior would not let him charge such ridiculous fees.

The depths of deception were astounding, and the financial loss was more than just numbers—it represented their future, their stability, and their chance at building their lives.

Louina wasn't just discovering financial exploitation; she was uncovering the deeper betrayal of trust that left her family vulnerable and powerless.

And so, the battle raged on—not just for their land, but to protect their dignity, their voice, and their right to exist.

I've spent a lot of my life feeling like my worth depended on how others saw me. Depression, generational trauma, and even my time in the Navy left me carrying the weight of others' judgments.

But the more I've educated myself, the more I've realized something crucial: my worth isn't theirs to define.

I am repeating the same battle as the Hickory family. They weren't fighting to gain respect or dignity. They already had those things. They were fighting to protect them, to reject the disregard forced upon them.

Their battle wasn't just for land or money. It was for their right to exist on their own terms and the right to define their own story, to be part of the world.

Letter from Attorney John D. Wakely to Superintendent Gabe E. Parker, Muskogee Agency — June 22, 1920, Pg 1

On behalf of Thomas Hickory, full-blood Creek 7963 National Archives, Fort Worth, Texas. Printed here in full for accessibility and historical clarity.

Tulsa,Ok.,June 22nd.1920.

Hon Gabe E.Parker,Supt.
Muskogee, Okla.

Dear Sir:

I am enclosing herewith the complaint of Thomas Hickory,a full blood Creek,3963,in which he complains that he and his children are kept out of their home,the farm of Jennie Hickory,adjacent to this City.

They have a good house there,and other improvements,and he and the children want to get into it.

The parties he blames for getting him out of the homestead,are J.G.Campbell who claims to have purchased the surplus 120 joining,and J.S.W.Bland,the Gdn of the Hickory children,and James M.Sykes,their Atty.

Hickory is running the streets an outcast;he came to me thoroughly skinned of everything available,except his own allotment;I have always objected to his wanting to sell his allotment,because his two younger children Sallie and Sammie are"too late" and I want them to get his land,or their interest in it,some day. The oldest child Louina is a girl of some intelligence,has been to school,and is able to keep house for Tom and the smaller children;but the parties in control of course want the whole 160,to plat into town lots,and Tom says they discourage him from getting back home,and drive him away.

Hickory has been destitute for years,and has been badly handled; I have matters pending in Court for him,and have often regretted meeting him as he has always been a source of expense to me,and I am compelled to lend him money,every few days.

I wrote Mr James C.Davis,Creek National Attorney about this Hickory family,and have never received a reply from him;I then wrote the Commissioner of Indian Affairs and he advised me to take the matter up with Mr Davis.

Is there any method whereby I can get the attorneys or officials of the Department of the Interior and of the Department of Justice to investigate the affairs of this Hickory family,to see how they have been treated.

Louina was in my office yesterday and showed me an account from Vandever Dry Goods Co charged against her,showing that in Nov 1919 while she was in school at Santa Fe New Mex, a bill for women's wear amounting to some $300, was run up. The bill shows such items as Teddy $10.50, Teddy $12.50,Teddy $15.00,Teddy $17.50, Teddy $22.50,and other items of kindred nature,all of which she says she did not buy.

Can you have the guardianship accounts quietly examined and experted as she is complaining to me that while she has no home,she ought to have

PHONES: OFFICE OSAGE 737
RES. CEDAR 1860

JOHN D. WAKELY
ATTORNEY AND COUNSELOR AT LAW
TULSA, OKLAHOMA

considerable money somewhere, judging from the number of sales of valuable lands which have been carried through against the Hickory family.

She also makes reference to an allowance of some five thousand dollars allowed as an attorney fee against the Hickory minors some time ago; and she states that she fears another similar allowance, by reason of a sale of her mother's land carried through against her wishes, and at the hearing of which she testified that she was present at her mother's side when the mother died, and that her mother's last wish was that the land in question be not sold.

Samuel C. Davis was formerly the guardian of these children, and when he came to his end at Joplin Mo. he was then under fire as the Gdn, it being charged by Mr John C. Boyd, U.S. Probate Atty at that time, that Davis and his wife Ethel Davis were holding deeds to themselves of the lands in which the children had rights, and which in fact all belonged to the Hickory children.

When Davis died, his brother in law, Mr J.C.W. Bland was appointed Gdn.

The lands in which the children were interested are as follows,

    Tuckabache
    Noa Tuckabache
    Tom Coney,
    Mose Coney,
    Lisa Coney
    Lucinda Hickory
    Jennie Hickory, ———————— all deceased allottees.
These lands are lost to the children, unless some investigation is had and attempt made to recover; some of the lands are immensely valuable.

It is indeed peculiar that this Indian and his children are homeless.

I am working on these matters, and with the influence of the Department I could shake them out.

I have the honor to be yours very respectfully

John D. Wakely

attorney for Thomas Hickory.

Letter from John D. Wakely, Attorney for Thomas Hickory, to Gabe E. Parker, Superintendent, Muskogee Agency, dated June 22, 1920. Pg 2

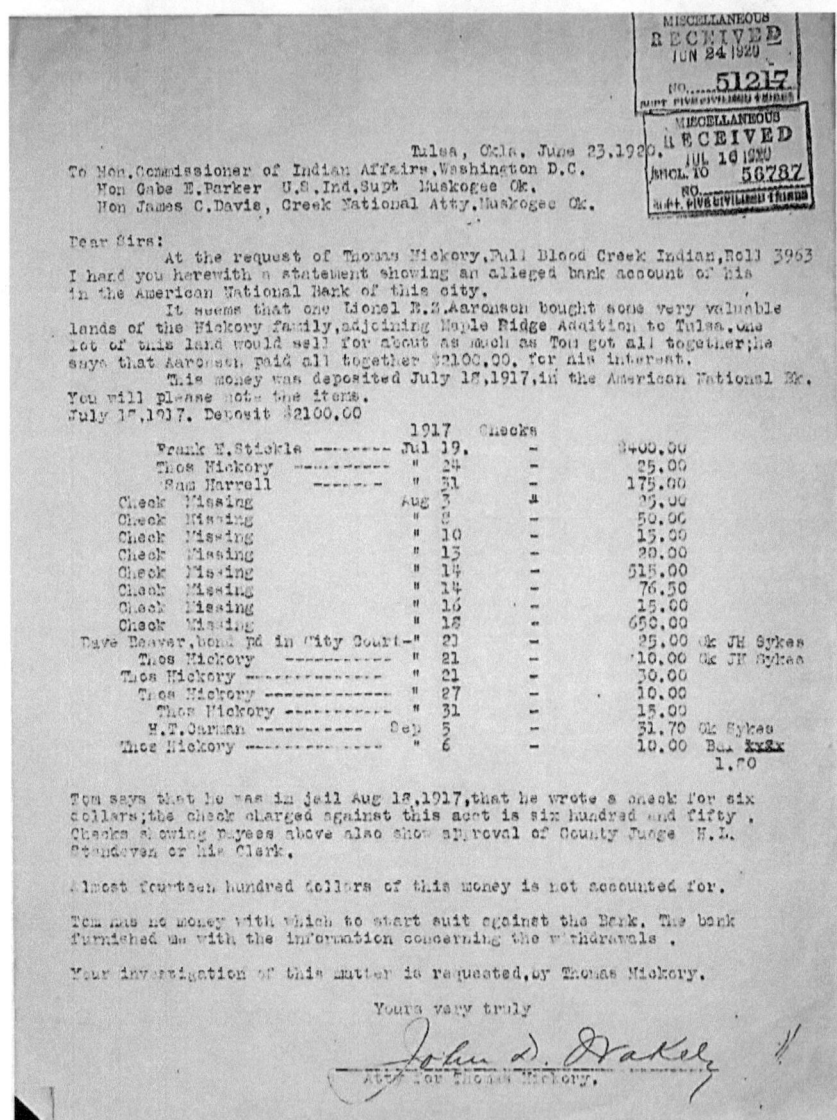

Reproduced and transcribed in full for accurate reading and preservation.

Letter from John D. Wakely to Gabe E. Parker, June 22, 1920 (NARA Fort Worth)

JOHN D. WAKELY
ATTORNEY AND COUNSELOR AT LAW
TULSA, OKLAHOMA

Tulsa, Ok. June 22nd. 1920.

Hon. Gabe E. Parker, Supt.
Muskogee, Okla.

Dear Sir:

I am enclosing herewith the complaint of Thomas Hickory, a full blood Creek, 3963. in which he complains that he and his children are kept out of their home, the farm of Jennie Hickory, adjacent to this City.

They have a good house there, and other improvements, and he and the children want to get into it.

The parties he blames for getting him out of the homestead, are J.O. Campbell who claims to have purchased the surplus 120 joining, and J.C.W. Bland, Gdn of the Hickory children, and James H. Sykes, their Atty.

Hickory is running the streets an outcast; he came to me thoroughly skinned of everything valuable, except his own allotment; I have always objected to his wanting to sell his allotment, because his two younger children Sallie and Sammie are too "lates" and I want them to get his land, or their interest in it, some day. The oldest child Louina is a girl of some intelligence, and been to school, and is able to keep house for Tom and the smaller children, but the parties in control of course want the whole 160, to plat into town lots, and Tom says they discourage him from getting back home, and drive him away.

Hickory has been destitute for years, and has been badly handled; I have matters pending in Court for him, and have often regretted meeting him as he has always been a source of expense to me, and I am compelled to lend him money every few days.

I wrote Mr. James C. Davis, Creek National Attorney about this Hickory family, and have never received a reply from him; I then wrote the Commissioner of Indian Affairs, and he advised me to take the matter up with Mr. Davis.

Is there any method whereby I can get the attorneys or officials of the Department of the Interior and of the Department of Justice to investigate the affairs of this Hickory family, to see how they have been treated.

Louina was in my office yesterday and showed me an account from Vandever Dry Goods Co. charged against her, showing that in Nov 1919 while she was in school at Santa FE, New Mex. a bill for women's wear amounting to some $300. Was run up. The bill shows such items as Teddy $10.50, Teddy $12.50, Teddy $15.00, Teddy $18.50, Teddy $22.50, and other items of kindred nature, all of which she says she did not buy.

Can you have the guardianship accounts quietly examined and experted as she is complaining to me that while she has no home, she ought to have...

June 22nd, 1920 (continued)

...considerable money somewhere, judging from the number of sales of valuable lands which have been carried through against the Hickory family.

She also makes reference to an allowance of some five thousand dollars allowed as an attorney fee against the Hickory minors some time ago; and she states that she fears another similar allowance, by reason of a sale of her mother's land carried through against her wishes, and at the hearing of which she testified that she was present at her mother's side when the mother died, and that her mother's last wish was that the land in question be not sold.

Samuel C. Davis was formerly the guardian of these children, and when he came to his end at Joplin, Mo., he was then under fire as the Gdn, it being charged by Mr. John C. Boyd U.S. Progate [probate] Atty at that time, that Davis and his wife Ethel Davis were holding deeds to themselves of the lands in which the children had rights, and which in fact all belonged to the Hickory children.

When Davis died, his brother-in-law, J.C.W. Bland, was appointed Gdn.

The lands in which the children were interested are as follows:

Tuckabache
Ned Tuckabache
Tom Coney
Mose Coney
Liz Coney
Lucinda Hickory
Jennie Hickory⎯⎯⎯⎯all deceased allottees.

These lands are lost to the children, unless some investigation is had and attempt made to recover, some of the lands are immensely valuable.

It is indeed peculiar that this Indian and his children are homeless.

I am working on these matters, and with the influence of the Department I could shake them out.

I have the honor to be yours very respectfully,

(signed)
John D. Wakely
Attorney for Thomas Hickory

Chapter 16

THE COST OF COURAGE:

It's time to move on…

The family fought tirelessly over the next several years to maintain some hold over their land. By 1926, the battle changed as they saw no way to save their family home. They sought at least a fair price for what remained of their land.

During this year, however, an unexpected incident shifted the family's focus: Thomas Hickory was hit by a car, leaving him seriously injured and hospitalized.

This seemed more than a mere coincidence. I felt it was an intimidation tactic, or even an attempt on his life, to break the spirit of an already struggling family.

Was this an accident? Or perhaps a distraction for the Hickory children so that the land deals Bland was forcing could go through. This would not be the last time that Thomas would have such an experience.

The doctor's report paints a grim picture: Thomas, about fifty-eight years old, had sustained a severe leg injury, with fractured bone shards that required surgical intervention.

But Thomas objected to the treatment. The doctor's notes hint at the struggle: he was "hard to manage," never having been [bedridden] before.

Thomas's resistance raises a question: Did he mistrust the doctors, suspecting foul play? He had every reason to. The poisoning of Indians was not a secret, and perhaps the trauma of his life had taught him to trust no one.

In the end, the infection spread and turned to gangrene, forcing an amputation. Thomas, unwilling to allow the doctors to cut off his leg, wished to live out his remaining days in comfort.

Louina appealed to the Department of the Interior, asking for all his money to be released—or, if that wasn't possible, at least $100 (about $1700 today) to care for him in his final days. The request was granted.

According to family oral history, our great-grandfather, Papa Hickory, fell asleep on a railroad track, and a train ran over his leg, severing it. Knowing what I know now, I can't help but wonder if this was an intentional act—a way to rid himself of the gangrene on his own terms, without letting the white doctors, whom he deeply distrusted, perform the amputation.

They had already taken so much from him: his wife, daughter, home, and money. He wasn't going to let them take his leg, too. This was something he could control. It must have been a calculated decision, as it worked. Thomas lived on, continuing his life with one leg, defying death and defying the forces that sought to destroy him.

L. C. NORTHRUP, M. D.
SURGEON
205 MASONIC TEMPLE
TULSA, OKLA.

August 27,1926

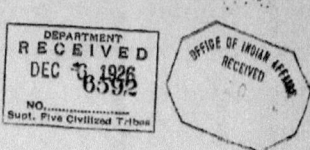

United States Field Clerk
New Wright Building
Tulsa, Oklahoma

Dear Sir:

Re: Tom Hickory

Tom Hickory is a man about fifty-eight years old.
He has been a hard drinker.

It is almost impossible to hold the broken fragments
in place without open operation due to the fact that the break
is so near the knee joint it is impossible to get sufficient
traction. The old man is hard to manage as he has never been
in bed. He objects to all splints and bandages. I believe
open operation with the metal bands is the easiest and best
method of handling this case.

It is sometimes necessary to remove these bands at a
later time. It may also be necessary to remove the third or
loose fragment if it is dead and will not grow. Tom Hickory
will be from six months to a year under my care. It may be
necessary to do more work before we get a perfect result.
However a good result can be expected.

My fee covers the entire surgical care of the leg
until recovery. I know this is a reasonable fee for work of
this kind in this locality.

Very truly,

L. C. Northrup M.D.

LCN:GE

Letter from Dr. L.C. Northrup to the U.S. Field
Clerk, August 27, 1926, describing Tom Hickory's
broken leg and difficult treatment.

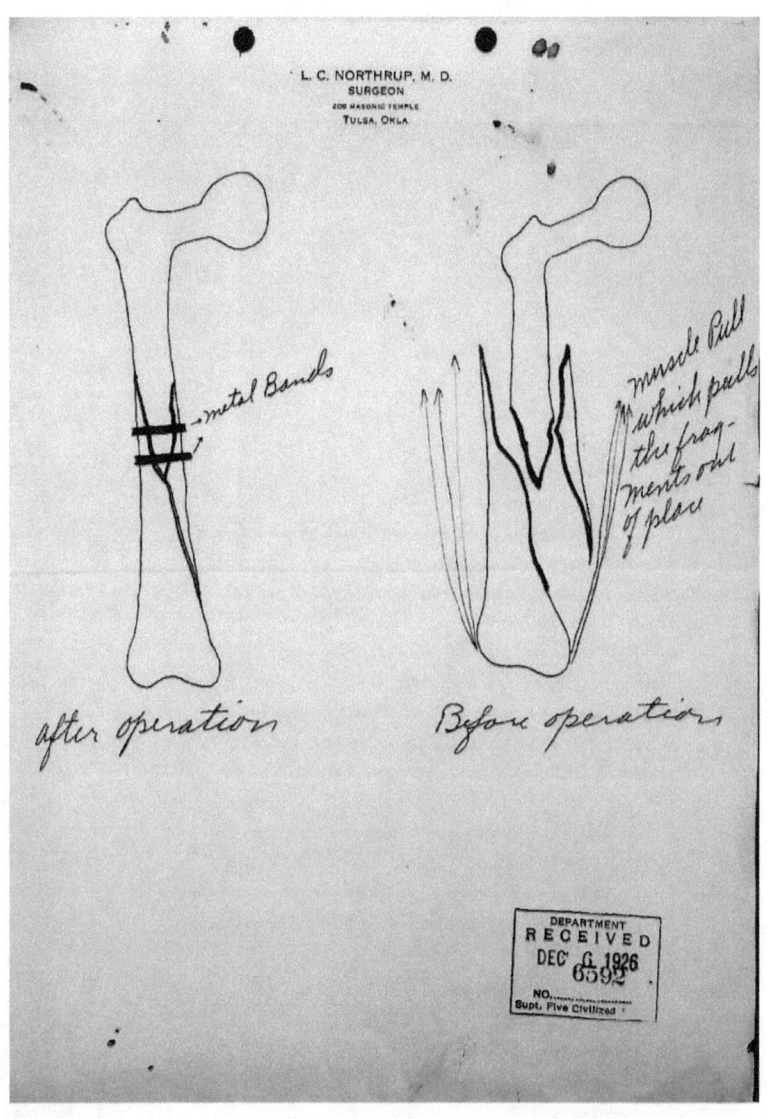

Sketch by Dr. L.C. Northrup illustrating the proposed surgery on Thomas Hickory's broken leg, 1926. The operation was never performed, as Thomas refused treatment due to mistrust of doctors.

Filed with the Office of the Superintendent for the Five Civilized Tribes, Muskogee, Oklahoma
National Archives and Records Administration (NARA), Fort Worth, Texas.
Printed here in full for accessibility and historical clarity.

[INDIAN SERVICE OF FIVE CIVILIZED TRIBES]

AFFIDAVIT OF LOUINA HICKORY SUNDAY
AS TO TOM HICKORY

I, Louina Hickory Sunday, of lawful age, being first duly sworn depose and state:

That my father Thomas Hickory had his right leg broken on the 17th day of August, 1926; that there was a compound facture of a bone and that the same has never knitted together; that a number of operations have been performed by the physicians who have handled his case since said injury.

That the physicians now advise me and advise him that unless his leg is amputated that he will die. That Thomas Hickory refuses to let his leg be amputated and if daily growing weaker from the poisonous pus that is in his infected limb.

That he is this day making application for the sum of one hundred ($100.00) dollars through the Field Clerk for spending money. That at the best he cannot live long and that he should be permitted to have such sums as he wants to spend. That he has over $17,000.00 in the office of the cashier and special disbursing agent at Muskogee, Oklahoma, and that in addition to that he has real property of the value of forty thousand ($40,000.00) dollars; that he has asked me to make this statement to the department so that they may be advised as to his wishes and requests.

Louina Hickory Sunday

Subscribed and sworn to before me, this the 23th day of March, 1927.

my com. exp.
Jan 15th 1929

This affidavit, sworn by Louina Hickory Sunday, confirms her father's deteriorating health following a compound leg fracture in August 1926. Despite medical warnings, Thomas Hickory refused amputation, growing weaker from infection. The affidavit also reveals that he held significant funds and real property at the time, underscoring how Native individuals—though technically "wealthy" on record—often lacked independence over their own money and medical decisions.

Chapter 17

They Were Not Silent—They Were Silenced

As the battle rages on...

The court cases and ongoing legal battles over the land have been complex and deeply unsettling to unravel. They were bullied, coerced, and forced into poverty through illegal and exploitative means. In my heart of hearts, I will always believe that many of my ancestors were murdered, though I know I'll never be able to prove it. That's why I call these events "red flags." At best, the speculators preyed on the family's grief, the youth of the children, and the language barrier faced by the father. At worst, they enacted a systematic and ruthless campaign of theft, manipulation, and murder.

The stress of this relentless battle must have taken a heavy toll on the children's education and well-being, forcing them to constantly worry about their father's treatment and the fate of their home.

Relocating was not as straightforward as it might seem. Like many other Native American families during the Allotment Era, the Hickorys discovered that their guardian had mismanaged their business affairs and spent their money, leaving them in debt. Although they unwillingly sold their property, they knew they had to decide to move on, but not without getting a fair price.

Campbell's initial attempts to acquire the Hickory family's land were driven by plans to develop what began as an average middle-class neighborhood. However, as the fight for the land stretched over the years, its value skyrocketed, transforming it into prime, wealthy real estate.

Despite this, Campbell sought to shortchange the Hickory family, paying them only a fraction of its true worth—a drop in the bucket compared to what had already been taken from them.

The Hickory children, like so many Native allottees, helped build Tulsa—not just by hand, but by checkbook, and not by choice, but through fraud.

Their inherited wealth paved roads, funded development, and lined the pockets of powerful men. Meanwhile, the children were thrown into poverty. The education they received from their inheritance wasn't one of privilege or higher learning. It was a masterclass in betrayal and survival. They learned, firsthand, how dark and deceptive the colonized world could be. And yet, they forged ahead with incredible tenacity.

My grandmother and her siblings weren't allowed to nurture their talents—neither in the colonized world nor in their Creek culture. Their past was destroyed, their present was hell, and their future was stolen.

How could they prepare the next generation for a world they did not know and could not trust?

I think of something as simple as piano lessons. That kind of privilege wasn't even a consideration—not for them, not for me. We didn't ask, "Can we afford lessons?" We asked, "How will we pay the bills?" "How do I best help my family?"

And maybe that would've been just fine if they had been immigrants who arrived with nothing. But they were not immigrants, they had land, they had money. And they were surrounded by opportunists, always ready to take. Their futures were hijacked—their birthright was stolen—

And the thieves got away with it.

As a society, we shrug it off. "Well, nothing can be done about that now."

Why not? If you've never experienced this kind of injustice, you might not understand how deeply it still lives inside us.

So, before you say, "That didn't happen to me," let me be clear: oh yes it did. It's still happening. And before you tell me about your uncle or your cousin and how they lost land too—remember this:

WE ARE INDIGENOUS.

This land was entrusted to our care. We thrived when we were allowed to care for it. Today, we survive. But so many of us have been denied the chance to truly thrive.

The Allotment Era absolutely shaped my life. And once I began researching it through my own lens, not through the lens of outsiders. When I did this, I could finally see that the story we'd always been told, was true.

One of the hardest truths to face was reading how my great-grandfather, Thomas Hickory, and his children were kept from the very home he built with his own hands.

They weren't just locked out—they were run off. Forced to leave the home they built, on the land they owned, treated like intruders in their own story.

How would you feel? I already know.

My family lived it.

My family carries it still.

The Crime of 1908...

The Indian Rights Association dubbed the Act of May 27, 1908,
as 'The Crime of 1908' due to the horrific effect the probate
conditions had on the Five Civilized Tribes.
The Allotment Era became a complex time
full of conspiracy and deceit,
including mysterious and untimely deaths.

They must hide the sullied transactions
of those so-called honorable men.

With land being traded, over and over again.

Quit claim deeds and general warranty deeds, "X's" and
thumbprints, interpreters and of course the greedy guardian!

Acting on behalf of the "dead Indian?"

Chapter 18

THE CRIME OF 1908

The imposition of colonization

I found it!

After years of research, I finally understood why so many Indians were dying before their time. In the records, it seemed almost routine: an Indian had to die before their land could be sold. It was too convenient, too patterned to be coincidence. I once called it the "Dead Indian Act."

In fact, the very structure of that system was made clear in 1908, when the Act of May 27, 1908, informally known as the Restrictions Removal Act, was passed. This law, disguised as a benefit to Indians, stated that when an Indian died, their heirs could have restrictions lifted and sell the land.

This allowed opportunists to legally strip land from Indian families, particularly those who were elderly, underage, or deemed incompetent. This created "dead Indians" which created "dead Indian land."

The Indian Rights Association dubbed this legislation the "Crime of 1908." [vii]

Section 9 of the Act May 27, 1908, made it plain [in part]:

"The death of any allottee of the Five Civilized Tribes shall operate to remove all restrictions upon the alienation of said allottee's land..."

It was an insidious piece of legislation. The guardianship system that was established, gave white men the authority to manage Indian land and finances, often without the landowners' full understanding or consent.

The court of law allowed men like M.F. Smith, Dr. JCW Bland, Sam C Davis, and many others to step in, make deals, and lease out land, all while claiming to act in the best interest of Indian landowners.

In Indian Country during the Allotment Era, a "guardian" was legally appointed to manage the affairs of an Indian ward, a minor or an adult deemed "incompetent" by the courts.

Unlike traditional guardianship rooted in kinship and care, these guardians often shared no relation to their wards, and appointments were based on enrichment opportunities rather than the welfare of the Indian individual.

While it might have been considered legal, it has to be questioned if it was ethical. Many guardians exploited their position, taking the resources from their wards, with little oversight or consideration for the devastating consequences on the Indian families they were meant to protect.

Many were involved in this corruption—among them, attorneys, guardians, judges, and local politicians. For the few that had honest guardians for your ancestors who preserved your interests…that is great to hear. The "dark reality" for so many was not a happy ending.

Oklahoma's Poor Rich Indians have stories that break your heart. [viii]

- A seven-year-old Choctaw girl starved to death, or possibly poisoned, though her estate which earned the equivalent of $4.5 million a year.
- One young Creek woman was declared incompetent because she spent too much money.
- Another was called incompetent for spending too little — too careful to trust anyone.
- Two weeks before her 18th birthday, a Creek girl was kidnapped and assaulted until she signed away her land.

Finally, there *was our* Lucinda Hickory, who died mysteriously just eight months after millions in gas were discovered on her land. General warranty deeds were being filed in Tulsa County Courthouse the very day she died.

These are only a small handful of occurrences from the Allotment Era. How many are out there who never realized the events surrounding the loss of their family's land?

ALLOTMENT ERA POPULATION CHANGES

Years	White	Black	American Indian	Comments
1890-1900	+288.40 %	+157.69 %	-0.02 %	Talk of free land and oil boom
1900-1910	+115.54 %	+147.13 %	+16.11 %	Oil Boom, Natives who have been separated from their tribes come back for land
1910-1920	+26.08 %	+8.57 %	-23.37 %	Crime of 1908
1920-1930	+17.00 %	+15.25 %	+61.72 %	The land is gone and Natives start living longer.

Complied by Verified News Network (VNN) 2024

Comments by The Lucinda Hickory Research Institute

Let's look at the census records. The above chart from my observation is the epitome of the Allotment Era. The Allotment Era reshaped the very makeup of Oklahoma. Between 1890 and 1930, white and Black populations soared with the promise of free land and the oil boom. For American Indians, the story looks very different. Having already lived on this land for a couple of generations, their numbers were never going to spike through migration. The census chart says it all. While whites and Blacks surged through migration and opportunity, Indians barely held on. And between 1910 and 1920 — the very decade of the so-called Crime of

1908 — survival itself faltered. The numbers prove what our families already knew: allotment was not just about land; it was about lives. A generation was stolen, not just in acres, but in blood.

Native "growth" barely kept pace with survival rates. The Crime of 1908 unleashed guardianship abuse, land theft, and suspicious deaths. While others prospered, Indian families were devastated. The numbers tell a story of loss: land, lives, and legacy diminished in a single generation. For those who endured, life became not progress but survival —it became — *"surviving 160 acres of betrayal."*

Louina Hickory Sunday (right)
and
Sallie Hickory Sunday (left).

Chapter 19

THE HOPE OF RECOVERY

Surviving 160 acres of betrayal

After spending their entire youth under the pressures of the *Crime of 1908*—or "progress," as it was called, the Hickory girls were now young women and married to Cherokees–the Sunday brothers. It was time, they hoped...to leave the past behind.

Louina and her husband William had already started their family, while Sallie and her husband Jess purchased some property on Sheridan in Tulsa, Oklahoma.

Losing their mother's land was a crushing blow, but they were finding themselves—perhaps for the first time—and had hope for a recovery. But just when they thought this Oklahoma nightmare was behind them, the past came sweeping down the plains in the form of court papers.

The Hickorys were being sued for a debt incurred years earlier by their guardian and attorney while they were still minors. Their "hope of recovery" soon faded, and while Jennie Hickory's land had already been taken, the consequences of that theft were far from over.

Though Dr. John Charles Willard Bland died on January 2, 1928, his actions—even in death—reached beyond the grave. The Hickorys girls now adults, are still burdened by decisions made during their childhood in a system that heard their voices yet deliberately disregarded them as irrelevant in the larger picture of "white progress."

One of the pressure tactics Sykes, Bland, and Campbell used to force the sale of the Hickory home was to pull in a Washington attorney, L.P. Summers, to petition for the removal of restrictions on Jennie's land. In Oklahoma, which was a routine, low-effort process— nothing that justified outside counsel. But they weren't looking for legal help; they were looking for cover. Another angle. Another excuse. Another way to pry loose a home the children were fighting tooth and nail to keep. They promised Summers $1,000 plus expenses, used his name to legitimize their scheme, and then—true to form—never paid him a dime."

With Bland now dead and Sykes still slippery, in 1931, Summers came calling—not on the men who had hired him—but on the Hickory family, demanding payment for a debt they had not agreed to, would have objected to, and never should have owed.

The Department of the Interior refused to release funds from the Hickorys' accounts to settle the claim, calling it an "exorbitant" amount. And they were right, but while the department guarded the restricted accounts, it did nothing to protect the family's other assets.

With the Depression deepening and the Bureau of Indian Affairs refusing to allow the Hickorys access to their own money, Summers instead turned to the only resource he could reach— to their shock, it was the land Sallie and Jess had just begun to call home.

After only five years of ownership, their property went up for sheriff's sale. It was another court battle that stretched over the next couple of years, costing time, effort, and peace. In the end, this too was lost.

All three Hickory children ended up living a simple life. All had small, modest homes. Before Louina died in 1951, she had a will drawn up that said her house was not to be sold until her youngest child was 18 years old.

My grandmother, of all people, understood how unforgiving *white* Tulsa could be to Indian families. In a city built on Indian land and guarded by white law, she fought to make sure her children had a roof over their heads until they could fend for themselves.

Before leaving Tulsa, Sallie's husband Jess Sunday had quite a career on the rodeo circuit in Tulsey

Town. He was a local celebrity. Given the opportunity, success was probable among Native people.

And once their land was gone, they were no longer a target and perhaps had some quality of life. But it came at great cost, great loss, and generational trauma.

Sallie and Jess ended up in a small house in Eastern Oklahoma built by Cherokee Nation.

Meanwhile, my Uncle Sam Hickory married a woman named Elizabeth, whom he loved and was fully devoted to for his entire life. He fought until the day he died in 1989 to recover the home that was stolen all so long ago. The home his mother left him.

Tulsa Daily Legal News, June 20, 1931. Legal notices like this one filled the newspapers, documenting cases against Indian families and their land. This clipping is part of a larger case involving the Hickory family, which ultimately led to the sale of their land.

Remembering Louina

Through it all, she remained a loving, steady presence, I never got to meet.

My mother always spoke of her like an angel.

In Creek culture, you take care of your community, and that's exactly what Louina did.

It didn't matter how much had been taken from her—it was always about how much she still had left to give.

Her concern extended beyond her own family to her neighbors, too. No one was to go hungry as long as she had something to offer.

Her community knew they could count on her, and one evening, a woman did just that. She came pounding on Louina's door—panicked, desperate, running from an abusive husband—Louina took her in.

Not long after, the husband showed up.

"Where's my wife?" he barked. "I'm coming in."

"No, you are not," Louina said firmly.

"Then tell her to come out here," he demanded.

"You're not going to see her. You go home and cool off," she replied.

He warned her: "Louina, you don't want to get in the middle of this."

But she stood her ground.

"I'll call one of my boys to get Bill Sunday," she said, referring to her husband.

And with that, the man left.

I don't know what happened to the young woman after that night. But I know this—for that one night—she was safe. My grandmother made sure of it.

When Louina passed, everything changed. Her death left a void that no one could fill. She wasn't there to guide her younger children anymore.

They had to raise themselves, relying only on what she had already taught them. And that absence—the loss of a true matriarch—was deeply felt.

The grandmother holds a sacred place in the family. She is wisdom. She is glue. She is the thread that binds generations.

My mother always spoke of her own mother as if she were a saint—always on a pedestal, always with reverence.

As the years passed, I noticed something: my mother never really had a chance to be a teenager with her. Louina died when my mom was in the fifth grade.

No one in the family ever said that out loud, but it's clear in the way my mother carried her memory—with both love and longing.

And still, even with such a short time on this earth, Louina left us with more than stories.

The court documents, the testimonies, the scraps of history that remain—they all tell us what kind of woman she was. Strong. Protective. Unshakable.

She was our matriarch, and even now, her strength is at the center of everything I am doing.

"The treatment of the Indian race in North America when traditions are handed down and when history is written, will be the most heartless, blackest, ungrateful and cruel pages ever penned by mortal man; it is a pity that our children may read it."

— *Isparhecher, Muscogee (Creek) leader, as recalled by Senator Muskrat of the Cherokee Nation,*
Welcome Address to the Cherokee Nation

Chapter 20

CUSTODIANS OF CORRUPTION

The dark reality of the Allotment Era.

Trying to get to the nuts and bolts of my great-grandmother's allotment has been the most complicated—and the most devastating—part of this work.

What I've uncovered isn't just mismanagement or misfortune. It's textbook <u>Allotment Era corruption</u> that is calculated, ruthless, and legal on paper, but rotten to the very core of humanity.

I'm sickened by the greed. Seeing a young Indian family taken advantage of in every way possible—land, money, character, and even childhood.

It's hard to say who carried the worst of it. Was it my great-grandfather, Thomas Hickory, whose name they dragged through the mud just to push him out of his own home?

Was it one of those who died too soon?

Or was it the Hickory children, forced to spend their youth and early adulthood—battling grown men so that they could keep a promise they had made to their dying mother?

Jennie Hickory fought to protect the land with every ounce of strength she had left. Her daughters spent their childhood and early womanhood fighting to keep it.

And Sammie—her youngest—fought until the day he died to reclaim what was stolen: The land his mother gave him. The land they were all told would be theirs.

Even now, the memory lingers. My mother once pointed out that land to me and said, *"You see all that? That used to be ours. But they stole it."*

How did she know that? Because her mother had told her. They had no real stability because the graft never stopped. This fight over the land went on for years. Even as little girls, the Hickory daughters pushed back because that's what Louina promised her mother. And when they became young women, they kept pushing because now they understood what had been done to their father and what was happening to them.

Who knows what Thomas was told? The records show he tried, again and again, to come home. And every time, they kept him out. They withheld his money. They withheld his land. He was a ghost to them.

And in document after document, I see the same names:

- James H. Sykes, attorney and Oklahoma State representative in 1914

- Dr. J.C.W. Bland, guardian, considered the first doctor in Tulsa

- J.O. Campbell, real estate developer

- Gubser, Linn, Standeven and many other judges

- David Beaver, full-blood Creek, fluent in both Creek and English, present at nearly every turn, starting with Tuckabache and maybe before that.

- Legus Perryman, former Chief of Creek Nation and turned real estate developer.

- Sam Davis — dead by the end of 1916, but his land dealings and influence lingered in the corruption that followed.

At some point, I had to stop and ask myself: Who was the good guy? Who was the bad guy? And who was just trying to survive?

The man who tried to help the Hickorys recover their land, Wakely? Was he good, maybe? But trying to take

50% of whatever he recovered. That's not justice, that's a hustle.

The bad guys are easier to name: While there are too many to call out here, I will mention these grafters: Bland, Campbell, Sykes, Davis, and the many judges. Men who profited from every loophole, every death, every lost inheritance.

But David Beaver... I don't know. Maybe he wasn't out to exploit. Maybe he was just trying to survive the Allotment Era the only way he knew how—by going along with the system, even if that meant turning on his own people.

That's survival, isn't it—doing what you have to, to survive?

These weren't just men doing their jobs. They were part of a machine that took advantage of a family while the law looked the other way. A full account of every crooked move these men made would double the length of this book. And even then, it wouldn't fully capture how relentless they were.

I don't know how they had the energy to be this underhanded for so long. But they did. And my family paid the price.

I've tried to give each of these men the benefit of the doubt. I wanted to believe that maybe they were doing what they thought was right, or that they were just caught in a system bigger than them.

But the deeper I go, the harder it is to keep telling myself that because the documents repeat it. Record after record, affidavit after affidavit, and petition after petition—it's all there. They weren't just doing their jobs. They were orchestrating this.

Sykes didn't just represent the family—he created confusion and exploited it as he controlled both sides of the legal table.

Bland didn't just manage the children's inheritance—he moved the pieces to weaken them at every turn.

Campbell didn't just buy land. He preyed on the young girls of an Indian family.

And the judges looked away during each illegal acquisition. Keeping a blind eye turned at every transaction.

They weren't uncertain. They knew! They were intentional.

And they don't deserve the benefit of the doubt. Not anymore.

The Inheritance...

I'm sure by now you must have guessed,
there was no inheritance left.

Look to Tulsa's Founding Fathers...
the oilman, the guardians, the grifters and the grafters,
because that is where our inheritance can be found.

Chapter 21

SMOKE FOLLOWS BEAUTY

The final years of Thomas Hickory

The forced sale of their mother's land, the loss of revenue from their great-grandfather Tuckabache's allotment, and let's remember the loss of Lucinda's life and her mineral-rich property—it was a lot to bear, but it was time to move on.

Both Louina and her sister needed to find a place for their own family now. They had hoped to purchase land together, but no matter what they tried, the hollow men thwarted them.

Their applications were approved, but only for separate parcels.

Both their perspective land purchases would eventually end in disaster, but I'm not ready to tell those stories—not yet—maybe not ever.

Right now, let's talk about the fire(s).

Now living on her father Thomas Hickory's original homestead allotment, at 15th Street between Yale and Sheridan, Tulsa, Oklahoma, Louina and her husband built a home to shelter their ten children and their extended family. William's mother, Neppie Sunday, and Thomas Hickory lived there too.

And at any given time, another relative might pass through the door needing a place to stay for the night. It was a house built on duty, love, and survival. It was now home.

Then...it caught fire!

They said it started in the kitchen. It was 1946, and my mother, Sallie Sunday, was maybe seven years old and home sick from school that day.

She remembered the commotion beginning, quiet, not panic, but definitely tension.

As the fire took hold, Louina—little Sallie's mother—was on the phone, calmly describing what was unfolding. Little Sallie, who had started down the stairs, turned back around when she saw her mother's lack of urgency.

It was her oldest sister, Louise, who finally shouted, "Mom, get off the phone! We have to get out of here!"

At that, Little Sallie's feet quickly picked up pace as she heads back down the stairs and out of the house.

They all made it out safely. But the house burned to the ground. With nowhere to go, Louina sent her children to Sequoyah Indian Boarding School in Tahlequah, Oklahoma, on the Cherokee Reservation.

My grandmother's reaction to that fire stayed with me. It reminds me of how trauma can dull urgency. People who have survived so much sometimes stop responding to new danger, because after a certain point, what's one more loss? It's not that they don't care. It's that they've come to believe they can survive anything, and when survival is the only goal, nothing else seems to matter.

After the house fire, Indian boarding school became Louina's answer for her children's safety. At Sequoyah in Tahlequah, her youngest daughter, Sallie, was only in second grade, still so small, she was placed in Home 3, and she remembered how frightened she felt—convinced she had been left there as an orphan. For her to even feel that way makes me wonder: what did the Indian children know at that time, what had they already seen, that this was her fear?

In Home 3, Mom said the house-mother did not like Indians. She was mean to them all. One day, as the girls stood in ranks, the house mother shouted at them, as she often did. This time, one of the older girls—her name was Wilhimena—talked back. The house mother retaliated, sending her upstairs to her room.

The house mother told the girls to stay put, and they stood stiff, afraid to move. Then it began. From upstairs came the crash of furniture scraping across the floor, drawers yanked open and slammed shut. Something or someone thudded against the wall hard enough to make the floorboards shiver beneath their feet. They could hear Wilhimena's voice raised in protest, then the sharp bark of the house mother's reply. The sounds tangled together—shouts, gasps, the slap of a struggle. For a moment it sounded like a storm tearing through the upstairs room. And then, just as suddenly as it began, it went silent.

When the house-mother finally returned, her hair wild and her blouse torn, she stormed into her office and slammed the door. The girls burst into laughter, their fear spilling out in giggles they couldn't hold back. But that laughter didn't rid the fear—it only masked it. For little girls, standing frozen in their ranks, this was how trauma planted itself: in the silence after the noise, in the not-knowing, in the lesson that adults could be dangerous and that safety was never promised.

Back in Tulsa, with the children at boarding school, Louina's husband, William, and some of his brothers converted the barn into a livable two-story home. What people today might call a barndominium— now a mark of trendy rustic comfort—was then born of necessity. For them, it wasn't a lifestyle; it was survival.

When it was finished, the children came home, and for a time, there was joy again.

About a year later, a traveling rodeo came to town. A big event—complete with Clydesdales! Jesse Sunday, William's older brother, a local celebrity on the rodeo circuit and square dance groups, got the family tickets. It was a joyful moment, and the family was excited to get the tickets that their uncle provided. This was going to be a great time.

On the day of the rodeo, the whole family went...all but one. Thomas didn't care for the crowds that would be present at events like rodeos. He stayed home. With the whole house to himself, he enjoyed the moments of solitude and began to take a long afternoon nap.

Lost in a peaceful sleep and with the family away, the house oddly caught fire...again. But this time, it didn't seem like an accident.

As the fire began to grow, Thomas was sleeping, and a group of white teenagers ran into the house trying to pull him out.

The commotion woke him, and disoriented, Thomas fought them off mistrusting their intentions.

After all...he knew their fathers.

But then he saw the flames. Realizing the fire was real, Thomas stopped resisting. With only one leg and limited mobility, he allowed them to carry him out.

Back at the rodeo, an announcement came over the loudspeaker:

"Would all members of the Sunday family please come to the front gate?"

When the family arrived, they learned what had happened.

Worried, the family rushed home to find, once again, their home in ashes.

And that was how the second fire began. That was how another home was lost.

Was this fire intentional?

What about the first one?

Answers we will never know.

It was about a year after the second fire–on August 4, 1948—when Thomas Hickory would have his final encounter with "white" Tulsa.

He was crossing North Boston Avenue in Tulsa, Oklahoma, when he was struck by not one, but two cars.

They called it an accident.
And maybe it was.
Both drivers were young white men.
Both were cleared of all charges.

The first car hit Thomas and threw him in the air. He landed 51 feet away and his crutch also flew into the air and landed on the side of the road.

The second car ran over him, hurling him another 36 feet.

The papers said he died "almost instantly." What exactly does that mean?

I think it meant he probably suffered…at least for a little while longer…

As his fight was over.
He was beyond their reach.
Their laws couldn't cheat him now.
The white man couldn't hurt him anymore.

Peace was waiting for him…along with Jennie, Lucinda, Tuckabache, and all the others taken by the treachery of the Allotment Era.

Today

Today, the deeds are all silent;
the titles are quiet.
All that is left now are
the echoes of Indian voices silenced.

Remembering the Allotment Era

When all was said and done, what remained was a complete disaster. We have already heard from the Indian Rights Association in Oklahoma's Poor Rich Indians, calling the Act of May 27, 1908, "The Crime of 1908." They described these actions as an orgy of graft, exploitation, and legalized robbery. Yet even that report only gave a glimpse of what all truly transpired during the Allotment Era.

In 1923, the Oklahoma Bar Association (OBA) passed a resolution denouncing the corruption in probate and guardianships. They described "the constant plundering of public funds by those who consider their certificate of election a license to take everything in sight," and the dissipation of estates through the appointment of unqualified guardians and administrators — some of them "graduates of the bankruptcy court," a pointed way of saying they had already failed at handling their own finances. Others were political allies rewarded with positions they could not competently fill.

The OBA painted a grim picture: two or more attorneys appointed at "fat salaries" to assist these guardians in their "faithful proficient performance" of duties — while the widows, orphans, and wards they were meant to protect went hungry and poorly clothed.

In this resolution they condemn the attorneys that took part in these heinous actions and suggested that the good attorneys took no part in this conduct. Yet instead of seeking justice, they merely "hoped" that it would all go away.

And yet, rather than calling for justice, the Bar expressed only this: *it is hoped that present conditions in our state may soon be regarded as unpleasant history to which none will care to refer, and that again we may point with pride to a State of prosperity and happiness.*

With that denial of justice, what they preserved was not prosperity, but *"A State of Corruption — Born by the Deeds of Dishonest Men."*

Well, I've never been to heaven, But I've been to Oklahoma. Oh, they tell me I was born there, But I really don't remember. In Oklahoma, not Arizona What does it matter? What does it matter?

—Three Dog Night —1971—Never Been to Spain

Chapter 22

IN THE ASHES OF THE AFTERMATH

We care and we shall refer:
Tulsa's unpleasant history

I was born in Arizona, but I really don't remember. I was raised in Oklahoma, and as I often say, I carry a rural Oklahoma high school education. I'm an autodidact and my life experience comes from the military. I wanted to go to college when I was young. Not now, in my sixties, as an old lady chasing a degree for the sake of it, but then—when it could have shaped my life, and my children's lives. When it could have made a difference in how I raised my family. I never understood why I was left out of the college plan.

I think I understand today. Because my mother was left out, too. And before her, my grandmother Louina was busy fighting for her land and then fighting to protect her children, knowing she would not be here much longer. And before her, my great grandmother Jennie didn't speak a word of English, and she too didn't have the luxury of planning it was about protecting what was hers. It wasn't in our family plan. Survival was our plan.

Louina did everything she could to secure her children's future before she died. She went to the Monsignor at Holy Family in Tulsa, who promised her, her children would receive a proper education. Her life experience encouraged her to leave a will for what remained of her property.

What remained of her property was something much smaller than all the land that she had fought to protect. Her 160-acre allotment, controlled by another man with the last name Campbell. And there was a simple house on Toledo, it did not have land— just a small yard, which was not to be sold until the youngest reaches the age of 18.

In her final days, she tried to give them the two things every family need: a foundation for stability, and an education to build their future.

Only a couple of Louina's children made it through high school. That was considered a success.

What they found at school was not belonging or opportunity. They found racism, loneliness, hunger, and a system that kept reminding them they were a burden because they were Indian.

There were other humiliations. Experiences that instilled the cruel idea that their heritage was not something worthy of pride.

As mom grew older, defiance took the place of shame. She began skipping school. When she faced suspension, her older sister Ruth convinced her to transfer to Sequoyah Indian Boarding School, where Ruth was already attending. Her sister promised it would be different than when she was little and that she would be able to watch out for her now. Mom agreed and attended Sequoyah. It was halfway through her junior year in high school but the change was a welcome one.

At Sequoyah, there was a measure of belonging. She wasn't looked down upon for the color of her skin. She excelled — senior class vice president, editor of the school newspaper. She was accepted. Yet even in that acceptance, she saw the limits of what was expected of her and every other Indian student: not excellence, but obedience. Sequoyah wasn't built to make scholars. It was built to make workers. It was not a traditional high school; it was a vocational school.

Sequoyah Vocational School

This is to Certify that

Sally Ann Sunday

has completed the Course of Study prescribed by the Sequoyah Vocational
School, and approved by the Oklahoma State Department of Education for
the High School Department and is therefore entitled to this

Diploma

Given at Tahlequah, Oklahoma, this twenty-ninth day of May, A. D.
One Thousand Nine Hundred and Fifty-eight.

Superintendent   Edwin S. Moore _Principal_

Diploma and senior class composite of Sally Ann Sunday,
Sequoyah Vocational School, Tahlequah, Oklahoma, 1958.
Sallie Ann, great-great-granddaughter of Tuckabache,
graduated as Vice President of her class. A diploma from
Sequoyah Vocational School, signed and dated May 29,
1958. A proud moment for her, yet a reminder that even
education was rationed. Vocational, not academic.

Now let's go to 1982. It was about two weeks before my own high school graduation when I was called into the counselor's office. She asked what my plans were. It was the first time anyone had asked me about life after high school. "Are you going to college?" she asked. I felt excitement rise in me, my posture straightening as I eagerly answered, "I would like to!"

That was when I learned my class ranking: "lower middle," she told me. To me, that sounded better than middle lower. But then came the real blow. "Have you taken your ACT test?" she asked. I gave her a blank look. I wanted to say yes, but I had to be honest. "What's an ACT test?"

She shook her head. "Well, if you wanted to go to college, you should have taken your ACT test."

I was later told that the Indian students were called in just before graduation, while others had the benefit of proper preparation. I don't know if that was true, but it felt true. My mother hadn't been prepared. Neither was I, therefore unable to prepare my own children. My idea of preparing them was providing them with a couple of pencils, paper, and a backpack. That was my part, their part was to show up on time, pay attention, do not disrupt the class and don't talk while the teacher is talking. Ahh, a sure path to success.

I knew the military. Two of my three children have or are currently serving. My oldest is a nurse. I'm very proud of them all. But none of their lives have come easy. The struggles of merely surviving are still there.

The struggle of knowing how to maneuver in the white man's world...they are learning.

Today, a younger generation is working to reclaim language, culture, and opportunity, but survival is not the same as justice. Their determination is resistance — not proof that the damage has passed.

Sometimes I feel the same kind of distance with them that I feel among my white colleagues. They are redefining what it means to be Indian. They avoid the word altogether calling it offensive, choosing something new every few years.

The first change I remember was when Indian became American Indian. Then more of our people went off to college, came back home, and told the rest of us were not "Indian" anymore. We looked at each other, well then, what are we if not Indian?

Native American...we are...Native American. That doesn't really work, because technically anyone born in America is a Native American. So, the pendulum swung again, this time toward Indigenous, connecting us with Indigenous people around the world. Maybe it's meant to sound informed, maybe it feels safer, or maybe it's a way to create distance from the ugliness we've lived through.

But in a Native community, we still call ourselves Indian. Especially those of my generation. It's not confusion. It's not ignorance. It's not offensive or politically incorrect, It's reality. It's what was lovingly instilled in our upbringing, it's who our parents and grandparents were — and ultimately, who we are proud to be.

I know some people feel the word Indian carries pain, and I respect that. But in my world, and in my family's history, calling myself anything else would mean stepping away from who my grandmothers were, from their struggle. It would be pretending they weren't enough, or that their identity needed correcting. I will not separate myself from my ancestors' journey because some European centuries ago made a huge geographical error. Being Indian is who I was raised to be.

I tell myself it isn't rejection, but change. Still, I wonder if the difference I feel is because this old wound of being crushed between two worlds still aches when I see them finding their place and I have yet to find mine. Change alone was bound to bring that kind of distance — it just didn't have to be so cruel.

But for the Hickorys, after years of court battle the Hickory family spent fighting for the foundation of their family, for their homes, their future—everything the government forced upon the Indian people—was taken in less than a generation. And for many, the connection to their community. Life became a scramble for survival.

But here, we care. And we shall refer. Because the story of Tulsa — of Oklahoma — isn't just about the crimes that were committed; it's about what we inherited in their place.

IN THE ASHES OF THE AFTERMATH

In the Ashes of the Aftermath, we inherited restlessness, anxiety, depression, poverty and the belief that nothing positive would last.

I think about that inheritance often. The grief we carry is quiet, it never leaves. It is heavy, and yet somehow, we still carry it — the fight, the memory, the unfinished search for justice.

We remain an "Indian Problem" when the same federal mindset that dismissed our ancestors' suffering still dismisses us today. Our own U.S. Secretary of Defense openly disregarded Native protest against the genocide at Wounded Knee. He elevated the men who massacred our Indian women, children, and elders to the status of heroes and closed the door on accountability with the line: "This decision is now final, and their place in our nation's history is no longer up for debate." He continued, "We salute their memory, we honor their service, and we will never forget what they did."

He is correct on one point — *we will never forget what they did.*

The genocide of the American Indian didn't matter then, and it doesn't matter now—not to the same government whose policies not only orchestrated our destruction but failed to finish it, yet they never stop trying. This shows how little has changed. We are not asking for political correctness; we are demanding historical accuracy and accountability. It's called *humanity.*

I watch how non-Natives claim our heritage through bloodlines of bondage, as if the pain of our ancestors becomes inconsequential to theirs. But slavery among Tribal Towns was never our identity. Many of our ancestors fought beside the enslaved, not against them. Some died for that justice, and still history blames the Indian instead of the policy that created the evil.

Perhaps it's time the United States government, the states, and every local municipality do what should have been done long ago: respect tribal sovereignty.

I set out to expose the corruption of the Allotment Era so that others might see just one of the reasons why we say—*you are on stolen Indian land.*

Through it all,

Oklahoma (*"Red People" in Choctaw*) remains my roots. It is my home.

Well, I've never been to heaven,
but I've been to Oklahoma...
What does it matter?
What does it matter?

It matters.

Epilogue

The dark reality of the Allotment Era is this:

Most Natives did not benefit from it—and many of their descendants are still unaware of why.

We were thrown into a world that did not want us, yet we were told we must belong.

We were taken from a world where we belonged, but now no longer knows us.

We were a family of wealth who lived in poverty.

We are a family of Indians who have —against everything—survived.

Afterword

The journey continues...

This has been a painstaking journey—one of uncovering calculated injustices against my ancestors. Not ancestors from some distant, abstract past, but the very people who shaped my present, my voice, the way I move through this world —and the way I carry my history.

Many want a happy ending to this story. I cannot offer that. I am told the happy ending is now—today—in a world where we have learned to survive in a colonized system, our culture reduced to a longing of what should have been.

The younger generations have learned to maneuver in this world, and some are reaching beyond survival. A few may even have the chance to thrive.

The journey continues...

I founded the Lucinda Hickory Research Institute—a small Native American nonprofit organization—where we carry the weight of generations and so we can tell their story. To support our work or share your family's story, visit us at;

www.allotmentera.com

Founded in 2020, LHRI exists to *uncover, discover, and recover* the true events behind land theft, untimely and mysterious deaths, and the silenced resistance buried in our ancestors' *Tales of the Allotment Era.*

It is time for big cities like Tulsa, and powerful Tribal Nations like the Muscogee (Creek) Nation, along with the state of Oklahoma, to reckon with this history. No good can come from covering up crimes against a people. The genocide did not end—it only changed form. To see it, you only have to be willing to look.

"Our present and future depends on a better recognition of the past."

—*Wes Studi, Cherokee Native, actor, storyteller, and Academy Award honoree*

Tatianna

About the Author

Tatianna K. Duncan is a U.S. Navy veteran, researcher, and storyteller dedicated to uncovering the truths of the Allotment Era. She served on active duty from 1984 to 1988 and later in the reserves until 2004, taking pride in both her service and the lifelong bonds forged with her shipmates. Like many people of color, she recognizes that military service was one of the few viable avenues to escape an oppressive system. It offered stability and discipline but came with the trade-off of opportunities she wished she'd had—like the chance to attend college. That dual truth—pride in service and awareness of what was denied—shapes the perspective she brings to her research and writing.

About the Author

A Mvskoke descendant of ancestors whose lands and lives were torn apart by the "paperwar" of manifest destiny, she founded the Lucinda Hickory Research Institute to preserve, document, and share the stories of Indian Territory; families who endured dispossession, corruption, and betrayal. Her writing blends memoir, archival discovery, and oral tradition, bringing family history into conversation with the wider story of Oklahoma and Indian Country.

Raised in Oklahoma, she carries both the burden and the resilience passed down through her grandmother, Louina Hickory Sunday, and generations before her. Her mission is to ensure their stories are no longer dismissed as "unpleasant history," but recognized as essential to understanding Oklahoma, Indian Country, and America itself. She continues to write, speak, and lead community projects that honor the memory of her ancestors while building a platform for justice and truth-telling for future generations.

Indian Territory: 160 Acres of Betrayal

Glossary

Allotment   The process by which communal tribal lands were divided into individual plots for Native citizens under policies like the Dawes and Curtis Act. For Creeks they received 120 acres for surplus and 40 acres for a homestead. Marketed as a civilizing effort, allotment was a tool of land theft, often resulting in the loss of Native lands and life.

Autodidact   A self-taught person; someone who gains knowledge through independent study and life experience rather than formal education.

Competency   A government label assigned to Native citizens to determine whether they could legally manage their land or money. In this book, being declared competent or incompetent largely depended on who was doing the bidding behind the scenes. Either way, it was a tool used for dispossession.

Creek / Mvskoke / Muscogee   These terms refer to the same tribal nation, but their usage varies by context. Mvskoke (sometimes spelled Mvskokē) is the traditional name in the Native language. Muscogee is the Anglicized spelling used by the federal government. Creek was a label given by European settlers, referencing the waterways near where the people lived in the Southeast. In this book, these terms are used to reflect both cultural identity and historical naming conventions during the Allotment Era.

Curtis Act (1898)   A federal law that extended the allotment process into Indian Territory to include the "Five Civilized Tribes". It dissolved tribal governments, nullified tribal courts, and paved the way for land allotment and statehood.

Dawes Act (1887)   The original federal law that authorized the division of tribal lands into individual allotments. It aimed to assimilate Native people and open up "surplus" lands to white settlers and developers. The "Five Civilized Tribes" were not included in this Act.

Fee Simple Patent   A land title that removed federal trust protections and gave an allottee full ownership on paper—able to sell, lease, or mortgage the land. After the Restrictions Removal Act of 1908, known as *The Crime of 1908,* it became far easier for Native lands to be converted to fee simple patents. This change opened the door for taxes, foreclosures, and predatory sales, accelerating the dispossession of Native families regardless of whether an allottee was truly "competent."

Five-Dollar Indian, A non-Native person who fraudulently obtained enrollment on the Dawes Rolls—often by paying a bribe or "five dollars" to an enrollment agent—during the allotment era (1898–1906). The false enrollment allowed them to receive land or other benefits intended for tribal citizens. Today the term is used to describe both the historical practice and, more broadly, people suspected of falsely claiming Native identity.

General Warranty Deed   A type of deed that guarantees the seller holds clear title to the property and has the right to transfer it, offering greater protection to the buyer. These deeds were more common in white real estate transactions and rarely favored Native landowners under guardianship.

Grafter *(expanded)*   A person, typically white, who exploited Native people during the Allotment Era through legal manipulation, fraudulent guardianships, and corrupt land deals. Unlike a simple con artist, grafters operated within systems of power—courts, real estate, probate—to legally steal land and wealth from Native families.

Grifter   A con artist or swindler who deceives others for personal gain. While some grafters were also grifters, not all grifters operated within the sanctioned legal and political structures that empowered grafters during the allotment era. The two are often confused, but grafter carries a heavier legal and systemic connotation.

Guardian   A person appointed by the court to manage the affairs of Native children or adults deemed "incompetent." In the context of this book, the term goes far beyond its legal meaning. While a guardian could sometimes be a Native child's own parent, the system became deeply corrupt when courts appointed White guardians looking for opportunity. These court-appointed guardians worked hand in hand with the judges, often enriched themselves through control over Native land and money, turning a supposed role of protection into a tool of dispossession.

Half-Breed, A person of both Native and non-Native ancestry. Historically used in U.S. law, treaties, and newspapers to classify people for land allotments, enrollment, and social status. Considered offensive today.

Heirship Lands   Land inherited by descendants of original allottees. These parcels became divided among so many heirs that ownership was fractured and easy to exploit.

Heirship Record   A court document listing the legal heirs of a deceased Native allottee, including family details like roll numbers, blood quantum, and dates of birth or death. Intended to protect inheritance rights, these records often became tools in probate processes that led to further land loss.

Homestead   The 40-acre portion of land set aside from an allotment for a Native American's individual primary residence. It was supposed to be protected longer from sale but was often lost through legal loopholes.

Indian   In this book, "Indian" is used intentionally to reflect the legal and historical language of the era. It refers to Native

Americans of federally recognized tribes, as defined by the U.S. government in the context of allotment and citizenship. I include this term with pride, as many of us—including myself—find no shame in being Indian. It is who we have always been.

Indian Rights Association (IRA)   A reform group of mostly non-Natives formed in 1882 to advocate for Native American rights. By the 1920s, the IRA exposed some of the allotment-era abuses, calling Oklahoma's probate system a national disgrace. Their investigation titled *Oklahoma's Poor Rich Indians* (1924) referred to the Act of May 27, 1908—sometimes called the Restrictions Removal Act—as *"The Crime of 1908."* Among those involved in bringing attention to these injustices was Gertrude Simmons Bonnin (Zitkála-Šá), a Yankton Dakota woman and powerful voice for Native rights.

Land Grabbers   Opportunists who targeted Native lands during and after the Allotment Era. Often developers, speculators, or grafters, these individuals manipulated legal systems, guardianships, and probate courts to obtain land from Native families under the guise of lawful transactions.

Mixed-Blood, A person of both Native and non-Native ancestry or of mixed tribal ancestry (for example Cherokee, Creek, Choctaw). Historically used—and policed—within federal and local systems tied to land ownership, enrollment, and identity.

Nene Estemerkv   Muscogee Creek for "Road of Suffering." This phrase is used to describe the forced removal of the Mvskoke people from their Southeastern homelands to Indian Territory. It captures the physical and spiritual toll of what is widely known as the Trail of Tears.

Probate Abuse   The legal manipulation surrounding the death of an Indian—rushed wills, forged documents, uninvestigated deaths—all used to convey land away from rightful heirs.

Quit Claim Deed   A legal document that transfers whatever interest a person may have in a property without guaranteeing title or ownership. It was often used in questionable or coerced land transfers from Indians to white buyers, offering little to no protection for the seller.

Speculators   Individuals or groups who sought to profit from the allotment of Indian lands, often by acquiring parcels at far below their true value.

Stolen Land — The land taken from Native people through deceit, coercion, fraud, and murder—acts later disguised as "legal" under the authority of the United States government. During the Allotment Era, federal policies such as the Dawes Act (1887), the Curtis Act (1898), and the Act of May 27,1908, made it possible for speculators, guardians, and government agents to strip Indians of their allotments under the pretense of law.

This theft was carried out not by strangers in the night, but by men in suits with deeds, probate papers, and guardianship orders. "Stolen land" acknowledges the deliberate, organized betrayal of trust and the destruction of Indian wealth through calculated exploitation. The alleged legality of those acts does not make them any less criminal.

It was called progress, but it was theft—sanctioned, signed, and sealed by the government that promised to protect us.

Surplus   The remaining 120 acres of an allotment after the homestead. This land was frequently the first to be sold or stolen once a person was declared competent or became deceased.

Trust Patent   Land held in trust by the U.S. government on behalf of an Indian. This was supposedly meant to protect Indian land, but even these lands were routinely mismanaged or stolen.

Glossary

Ward   An Indian legally placed under the authority of a guardian. Wards were stripped of autonomy over their own land, finances, and often their bodies, under the guise of protection.

White Man   Used in historical and narrative context, not as a slur. Refers to settler society and the white power structure responsible for implementing and profiting from policies that dispossessed Indians of land, family, and agency.

Documents of Evidence and Citations

---

i Probate Record, In the Matter of the Estate of Tuckabache, Probate No. 777, County Court of Tulsa County, Oklahoma, May 17, 1910.

ii The biography of L.C. Perryman, Tulsa, Oklahoma by Reuben L. Partridge

iii The biography of L.C. Perryman, Tulsa, Oklahoma by Reuben L. Partridge

iv *Probate Record, In the Matter of the Estate of Tuckabache, Probate No. 777,* County Court of Tulsa County, Oklahoma, May 17, 1910.

v Tulsa County Court, *Petition for Letters of Guardianship in the Matter of Thomas Hickory and Jennie Hickory, Incompetents,* Probate No. 1344, filed January 17, 1913, Tulsa County, Oklahoma, Clerk of the County Court, E. B. Irvan.

vi Supreme Court of Oklahoma, *In re Hickory's Guardianship. Hickory et al. v. Campbell et al.,* 75 Okla. 79, 182 P. 233 (1919), No. 10554, decided June 17, 1919 (statement of Louina Hickory)

vii *Indian Rights Association.* **Oklahoma's Poor Rich Indians: An Orgy of Graft and Exploitation of the Five Civilized Tribes, Legalized Robbery.** Philadelphia: Indian Rights Association, 1924.

viii *Indian Rights Association.* **Oklahoma's Poor Rich Indians: An Orgy of Graft and Exploitation of the Five Civilized Tribes, Legalized Robbery.** Philadelphia: Indian Rights Association, 1924.